"Old Ironsides"

Colin Stewart • Jean Costelloe

CP

Cornerstone Publishing
Rathdrum, Co. Wicklow
Ireland

First Published 2001

by

CORNERSTONE PUBLISHING
Rathdrum, Co. Wicklow
Ireland

First Edition

Printed in Ireland by
Ross Print Services Ltd.
Greystones, Co. Wicklow.
Tel: +353 1 287 6612

A catalogue record for this book is available from the British Library.

ISBN 0-95406140-3

Copyright ©
Colin Stewart • Jean Costelloe

Every effort has been made to identify all copyright holders.
The publisher would be happy to rectify any omissions
at the earliest opportunity.

All rights reserved. No part of this book may be reproduced or utilised in any form or by any means electronic or mechanical, including photography, filming, recording, video recording, photocopying or by any information storage and retrieval system, or shall not by way of trade or otherwise, be lent, re-sold or otherwise circulated in any form of binding of cover other than that in which it is published, without prior permission in writing from the publisher. Any person who does any unauthorised act in relation to this publication may be liable to criminal prosecution and civil claims for damages. The moral rights of the author have been asserted.

Acknowledgement

The authors wish to acknowledge the help of the Department of the Navy, U.S. Naval Academy Museum, Annapolis; of the United States Naval Institute, Annapolis; of Plymouth Naval Library, Devon; of the Bordentown Historical Society, Bordentown, New Jersey; of the **USS Constitution** Museum, Boston, Massachusetts; of the Alabama Historical Association, Birmingham, Alabama; and Coillte Teoranta (The Irish Forestry Board).

Thanks are also due in no small measure to Peter Ede, Specialist Skipper Technician, of the University of Plymouth, Devon, for technical advice, and proofreading; and to Adam Stewart, for the initial layout and presentation.

While there were several sources of reference available to us in writing this book, where Charles Stewart's family life was concerned, none was referred to more frequently than Jane McL. Côté's comprehensive *Fanny and Anna Parnell*.

Colin Stewart	Jean Costelloe
Soar, Devon	Avondale, Wicklow

June 2001

Build me straight, O worthy Master!
    Stanch and strong, a goodly vessel,
That shall laugh at all disaster.
    And with wave and whirlwind wrestle!

        H.W. Longfellow: The Building of a Ship

"Old Ironsides"

The story of a man and a ship
- their names linked forever
in the history of the American Navy.

The man,
Charles Stewart
- grandfather of the controversial
Irish Home Rule politician Charles Stewart Parnell

The ship,
the *USS Constitution*
- monument to an age of piracy
and excitement on the high seas!

Part of Family Tree

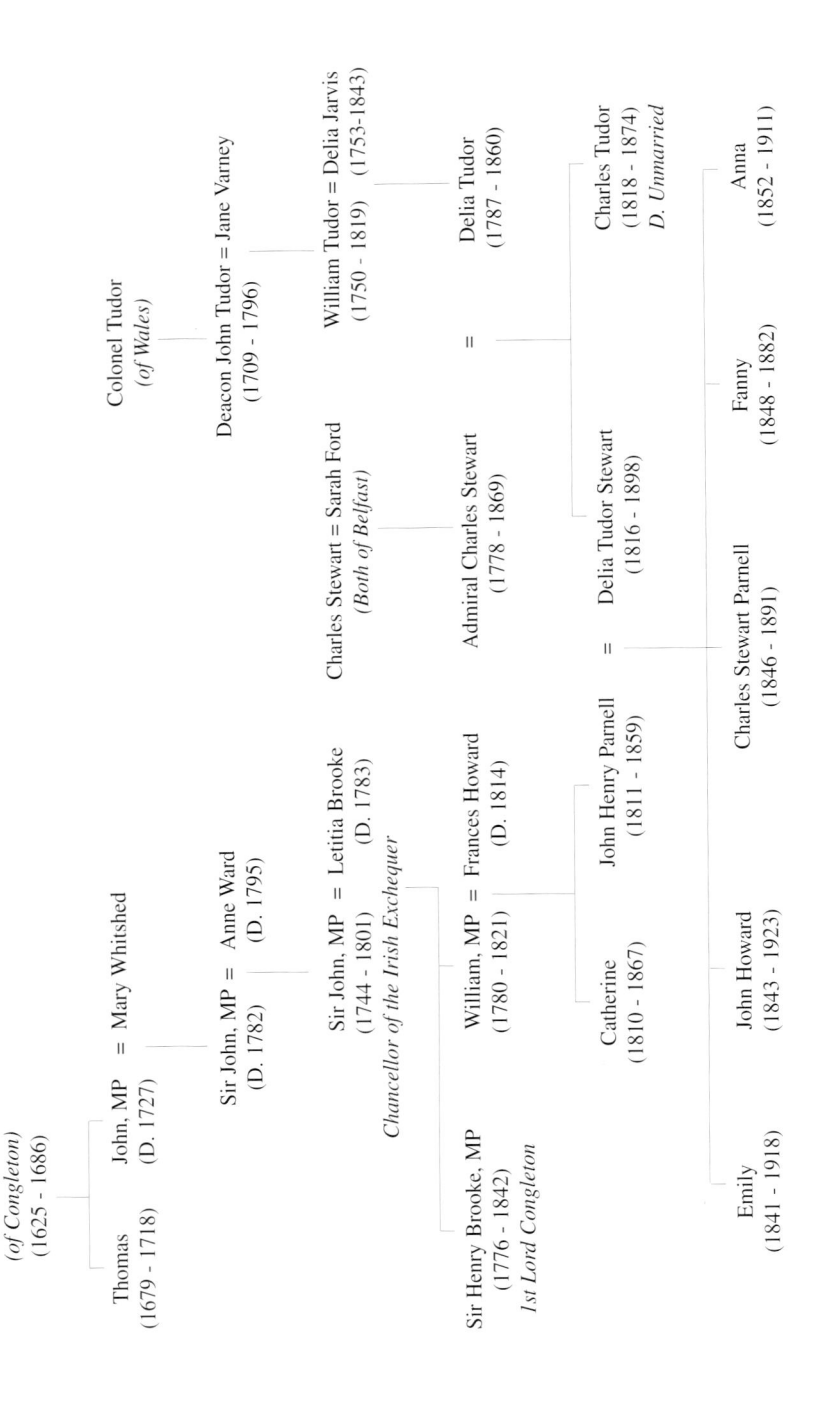

Thomas Parnell
(of Congleton)
(1625 - 1686)

Thomas
(1679 - 1718)

John, MP = Mary Whitshed
(D. 1727)

Sir John, MP = Anne Ward
(D. 1782)   (D. 1795)

Sir John, MP = Letitia Brooke
(1744 - 1801)   (D. 1783)
Chancellor of the Irish Exchequer

William, MP = Frances Howard
(1780 - 1821)   (D. 1814)

Sir Henry Brooke, MP
(1776 - 1842)
1st Lord Congleton

Catherine
(1810 - 1867)

John Henry Parnell
(1811 - 1859)

Colonel Tudor
(of Wales)

Deacon John Tudor = Jane Varney
(1709 - 1796)

William Tudor = Delia Jarvis
(1750 - 1819)   (1753-1843)

Delia Tudor
(1787 - 1860)

Charles Stewart = Sarah Ford
(Both of Belfast)

Admiral Charles Stewart
(1778 - 1869)

=

Delia Tudor Stewart
(1816 - 1898)

Charles Stewart Parnell
(1846 - 1891)

Charles Tudor
(1818 - 1874)
D. Unmarried

Emily
(1841 - 1918)

John Howard
(1843 - 1923)

Fanny
(1848 - 1882)

Anna
(1852 - 1911)

One

Charles Stewart

The story of how Charles Stewart ran away from home, began his life at sea as a cabin boy, and rose to become an admiral, has all the romance and excitement of the classic adventure novel.

On this stormy passage he risked his life repeatedly and became a celebrated war hero, was fêted by presidents, and lauded by Congress. When his reputation as an officer was threatened and he faced public humiliation, he exonerated himself completely; so successfully in fact that he was later considered a suitable candidate for the highest political office in the land!

He lived at arguably one of the most exciting times in American history, and the way he lived his life was truly representative of the age. A sense of fearlessness abounded which he and some of his contemporaries displayed time and again; they were a breed born of a new land, and it fell to them to make a stand against the oppression of old regimes, or submit.

Stewart had a great respect for the rights of Man, was vigorous in his condemnation of abuses of liberty, and was prepared to fight to see justice prevail. It can be no fluke that the sense of outrage he felt against certain acts of oppression was to manifest itself just as passionately in his grandson, Charles Stewart Parnell, in his fight for Home Rule in Ireland.

Charles Stewart was born of pioneering stock and displayed that unique brand of courage all his life. A man held in high esteem by presidents and seamen alike, he tried to enlist to fight in the Civil War, at the age of 83! That alone gives some insight into the mystique of the man known as "Old Ironsides".

Charles Stewart

In the Midst of the Revolution

The first shots of the American Revolution were fired at the Battle of Lexington and Concord on 19 April 1775, and so began a war which was to last for eight years, and smoulder on in varying degrees of intensity for another thirty after that.

Charles Stewart was born in Philadelphia on 28 July 1778, the month after the British troops evacuated the city. He was the youngest of the eight children of Charles Stewart and his wife Sarah (née Ford), Irish emigrants from Belfast.

His father died before he was two, leaving his mother still with four children to provide for, and with limited means for their support and education. In time she would meet and marry Captain Britton, a commander of George Washington's bodyguard.

Growing up in the city where the Schuylkill River joins the Delaware and flows into the Delaware Bay, the young Stewart soon set his heart on going to sea. At the age of 13, he responded to parental opposition by running away from home. He was unsuccessful and was forced to return, but Captain Britton accepted the inevitable and did what he could to help the boy in his chosen career.

Stewart joined the United States merchant service as a cabin boy and began his life at sea, working his way up through the grades to the command of an Indiaman, engaged in trade with the East Indies. It was in this position, when he stood poised to be successful in the mercantile marine, that he decided to join the embryonic United States Navy.

On 9 March 1798, he was commissioned a lieutenant in the navy and received orders to join the frigate *USS United States*, then under the command of Commodore John Barry.

The United States Navy

After the Revolution, in the fervour of their newfound status as republicans, few Americans saw the need for sea power to keep their land free. A permanent navy was perceived as an instrument of war, as wielded by the kind of tyrannical regime they had just fought to expel.

For that reason, in 1785, there was no opposition to the sale of the frigate *Alliance*, the last of the fleet assembled by George Washington while under British rule. But shortly after this, when Algerian pirates seized 23 American seamen it was the ransom demanded for their release more than measures to prevent further outrages that troubled Congress.

The unpredictability of the despotic Dey of Algiers, ruler of the most powerful of the Barbary Coast States (the others being present-day Morocco, Tripoli, and Tunisia), was well-known, and made the safe return of the hostages unlikely.

At that stage, John Adams, as Ambassador in London, exchanged letters with Thomas Jefferson, Ambassador to France, in which he advocated surrender. Jefferson favoured the building of a fleet and tackling "these nests of Banditti", but his idea was seen as too radical at the time.

Birth of a Navy

Seven years later the French Legislative Assembly declared war on Austria, but it was not until Britain joined the conflict, in April 1793, that President Washington proclaimed the United States' neutrality. However, this was often infringed, and with attacks on merchant shipping by the Algerians continuing, Washington recommended the building of six frigates.

In May 1793 France authorised seizure of cargo bound to enemy ports in neutral ships. This act angered the United States, and so began a long and bloody war between the two countries.

Although Thomas Jefferson had previously favoured aggressively pursuing the Barbary Coast pirates, his Republican colleagues, representing inland areas, saw little point in voting for the construction of warships. On 27 March 1794, Congress eventually passed an act intended to prevent and punish the depredations of the Algerian pirates. It was a compromise, in that while it authorised the building of six frigates, if the war with the Algerians was resolved beforehand the order would be cancelled.

The authorisation called for four ships of 44 guns each - the ***United States***, ***Constitution, President***, and ***Chesapeake***, and two of 36 guns - ***Constellation*** and ***Congress***. (This was later amended when the battery of the ***Chesapeake*** was changed, and there were three ships of each class built.)

The matter was referred to Henry Knox, Secretary of War. He in turn accepted the plans of Joshua Humphreys of Philadelphia. Humphreys prepared the models of six ships which, when built, were unquestionably the finest of their class afloat.

*The **United States** at her commissioning ceremony in 1797. Charles Stewart was a midshipman on her maiden voyage.*

Two

Lieutenant Charles Stewart

The *United States* was the first of these ships to be launched, in May 1797, in Philadelphia. After her commissioning ceremony, she was equipped and set sail on her maiden voyage in March 1798. On board were three young midshipmen who had become good friends during training: First Lieutenant Charles Stewart, Third Lieutenant Richard Somers, and Fourth Lieutenant Stephen Decatur. All three were to prove themselves heroic.

Born in 1779, at Sinepuxent, Maryland, Decatur was the son of a naval captain. Despite his youth, by the time he went to sea, he already had a reputation for being fearless. Even at that age he had partaken in several duels. He was an excellent shot and always aimed to wound an opponent. Somers was born in Cape May, New Jersey, the son of an officer in the Continental Army.

One anecdote which survives in some accounts gives an insight into the culture of bravado which fuelled the fearlessness of these young men. Once, in the company of other junior officers, Decatur called Somers a fool. Decatur apologised and Somers readily accepted it, only to be ostracised by the other officers who thought him cowardly for being so forgiving. Somers felt he had no choice but to challenge all six men present to duels. Decatur quickly offered his services as Somers' second.

Somers' first opponent wounded him in the right arm, and the next shot him in the thigh. Somers refused Decatur's offer to take the pistol and continue in his place. He wounded the next man and at this point the duel was unanimously concluded, Somers restoring his honour.

Lieutenant Stewart remained on the ***United States*** for over two years, while the ship was used in the West Indies, to restrain the French privateers. She was successful in this, and also in protecting American merchant ships against piracy.

She was then engaged in carrying various diplomats to France for the purpose of agreeing treaties between the two countries and Stewart was denied the chance to be more actively utilised.

This situation did not last for long and, on 16 July 1800, he was appointed to the command of the schooner ***Experiment***, 12 guns, in which he sailed on a tour of duty to the West Indies.

*John Barry, captain of the **USS United States***

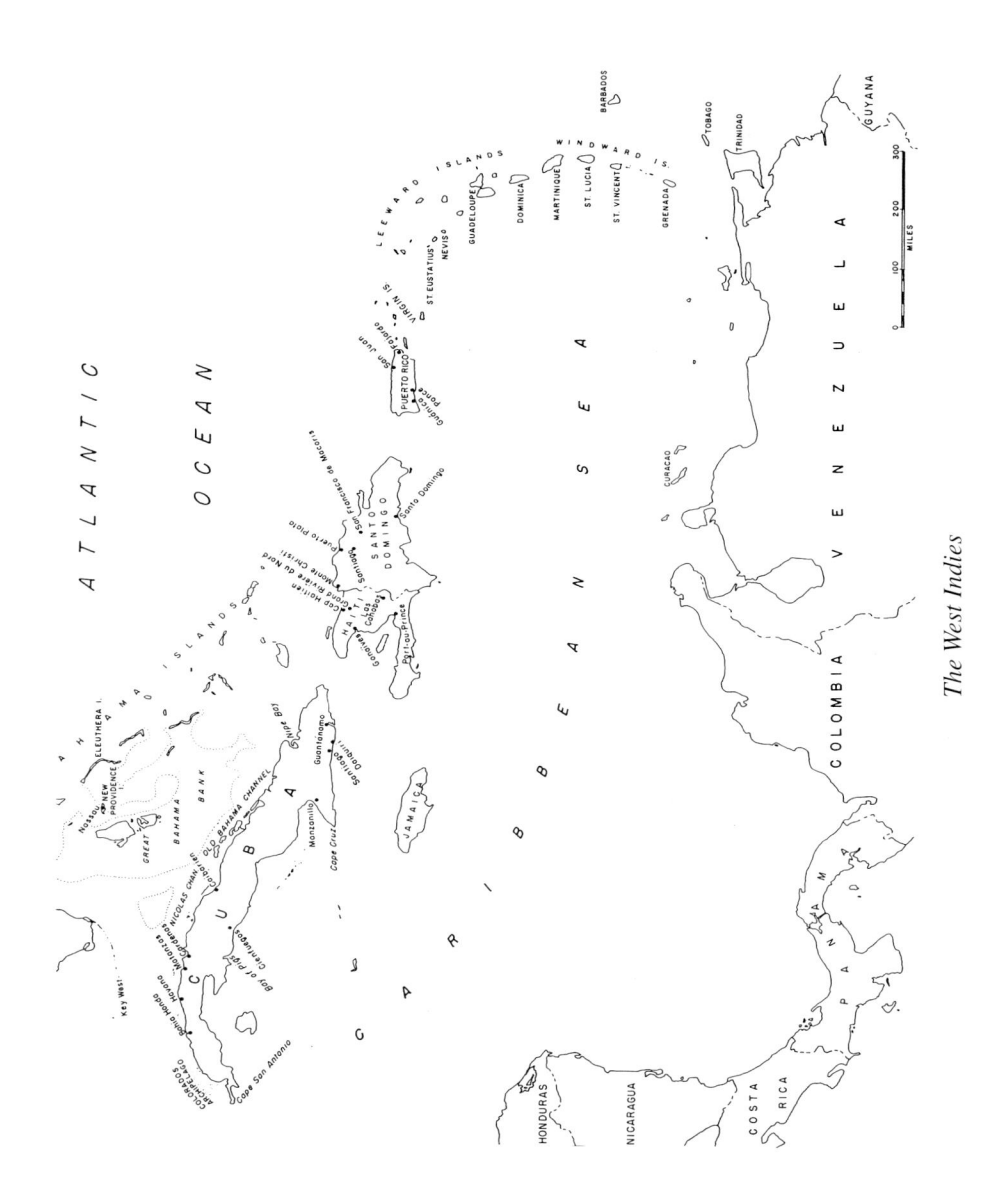

The West Indies

USS Experiment

On the night of 1 September 1800, Stewart confronted the armed French schooner ***Deux Amis***, and brought her into action, which ended within ten minutes. Upon her surrender, Stewart promptly sent his "prize" to the United States. (The custom of the day was that captured enemy ships, and their contents, were sold at auction, the spoils being divided between officers and crew, the captain always receiving a large proportion.)

After this, while cruising off Barbuda, on 30 September, two ships were seen bearing down on the ***Experiment***, with all sails set and English colours hoisted. The ***Experiment*** remained lying to, with the British signal of the day flying, until the ships were within range and Stewart saw that one was an 18-gun brig-of-war, the other a three-masted schooner of 14 guns. Neither would answer his signal.

Stewart retreated from such superior force, and waited for the possibility to separate them. His schooner outsailed them and, after a fruitless chase of two hours, they gave up, hoisted French colours, fired a gun in defiance, and sailed away.

Now aware of their intention and power, Stewart manoeuvred the ***Experiment*** so that he was in their wake, and his became the pursuing vessel. That evening he came upon the three-masted schooner and, taking a position on her port quarter, poured in a broadside; within minutes, she struck her colours, and surrendered.

She was the French schooner ***Diana*** and, while the accompanying brig made good her escape, Stewart dispatched his prize to the United States. After this he continued to cruise the area and recaptured a number of American vessels which had been taken by the French, and thus recovered a large amount of booty from the privateers.

Incident off Barbuda

On the night of 16 November, the ***Experiment*** came upon an armed vessel and, after repeatedly hailing her to heave to, that a boat might go alongside, and ascertain her intentions, when he received no response, Stewart opened fire.

The vessel began a running fight with great spirit for forty minutes, until she became so badly damaged by the ***Experiment***'s fire, that she had little choice but to strike her colours, and submit.

She was the British schooner *Louisa Bridger*, armed with eight nine-pounders. The encounter came about because both captains believed the other craft to be French. When Stewart saw the damage his shots had inflicted he ordered all his officers and crew to assist in repairing the worst of it.

*The **Experiment** and the British **Louisa Bridger** in battle at night. Lieutenant Stewart believed her to be French.*

The Visit to Santo Domingo

After this Stewart sailed to St Kitts, where he was ordered to proceed with a convoy from Martinique to the island of St Thomas. He was then to go to Curacoa, to look for the brig *Pickering*, the frigate *Insurgent*, and their store ship, all three feared lost in equinoctial gales.

Stewart found no trace of these, but it was while he was on the return journey, on course for Norfolk, Virginia, that he found a craft in distress, being lashed on the reef off Saona Island. Seeing that there were people aboard her and that only a small part of her quarter deck remained above water, he anchored the *Experiment* as near as he could and sent boats to the rescue.

There were some sixty women and children on board, with seven members of crew. They were trying to escape from a rebel siege in Santo Domingo, in the Dominican Republic, and had been on the rocks for two days without food or water.

Stewart took all survivors aboard the *Experiment* and set sail for Santo Domingo, where they landed next day. The gratitude of the inhabitants was overwhelming and the President, Don Joaquin Garcia, wrote to President Jefferson commending in the highest terms the conduct of Lieutenant Stewart and his gallant crew.

A Change of Enemy

In February 1801, the Quasi-War with France ended, but by the time the news was conveyed to the American fleet there was a new conflict looming. In May, the Pasha of Tripoli, deciding that the amount of tribute being paid to him was insufficient, declared war on the United States.

Meanwhile, upon her arrival in Norfolk, the *Experiment* was taken out of service and sold off. Under an act of Congress fixing the Naval establishment, Stewart was among 36 lieutenants retained, and was put in charge of the frigate *Chesapeake* while she was docked in port there.

In 1802, he joined the frigate *Constellation* as first officer of Captain Alexander Murray, who had been ordered to Tripoli. This was a short cruise of a year, offering him little opportunity for distinction, the only incident of note being on 22 July, when the *Constellation* engaged a Tripolitan galley and eight gunboats, sinking two.

On his return, Stewart was given command of the brig *Syren*, 16 guns, then being built at Philadelphia. Once she was equipped and launched, she sailed for the Mediterranean to join the command of Commodore Preble, to provide protection for American merchant shipping.

The rendezvous for the squadron was Syracuse, on the island of Sicily, and when Stewart arrived he found that a major crisis had developed. The frigate *Philadelphia*, under Captain William Bainbridge, had been in pursuit of an enemy ship, and had run hard aground on an uncharted reef just outside Tripoli harbour. All attempts to free her - including jettisoning her cannons - had failed, and when Tripolitan gunboats surrounded her, Bainbridge had to surrender, and 307 officers and men were taken captive. A few days later the Tripolitans towed the ship into the harbour.

Now in Syracuse, Stewart was reunited with his old friend Stephen Decatur, and together they masterminded a plan to destroy the *Philadelphia*.

Decatur elected to go in the ketch *Intrepid* with seventy men, several of whom were disguised as Maltese fishermen. Their objective was to recapture

Captain Stephen Decatur, by Olivio Sozzi, 1805

*The **Philadelphia** burns while Stephen Decatur and crew escape under the **Syren**'s covering fire.*

the frigate, rig explosives, fire the ship, and escape - all before the guards in the nearby Tripolitan fort realised what was happening. The *Syren*, under Stewart, lay close by to provide covering fire once the alarm was raised. In the event, when the guards realised what was happening there followed a heavy and frantic exchange of fire, but the mission was successful and only one of the men was wounded. For his part in what Lord Nelson called "the most daring act of the age", Decatur was promoted to the rank of captain, and to this day he remains the youngest man ever to hold that rank.

The Blockade of Tripoli

After this successful mission, Lieutenant Stewart, with the *Syren*, *Vixen*, *Enterprise*, and *Nautilus*, all under his command, enforced a rigid blockade of the city of Tripoli and adjacent harbours. During this blockade he frequently led vessels from the cordon to attack the batteries and flotilla, to force the Tripolitans to use their ammunition.

During one of these forays Stewart captured the brig *Transfer* off Tripoli. She was taken into the United States service and renamed, appropriately, *Scourge*. The following day, 22 March 1804, he captured the polacre *Madonna et Catapaliari*.

On 21 July 1804, Commodore Preble arrived off Tripoli with the *Constitution*, prepared for battle. He had in his squadron some of the best young officers in the navy, including lieutenants Decatur, Stewart, Richard Somers, Isaac Hull, and John Smith; none of whom was over thirty. These, along with Captain William Bainbridge (at that time being held prisoner in Tripoli), would become known in history as "Preble's Boys."

On 3 August, the wind favourable, Preble set about attacking the town, the flotilla, and the batteries of Tripoli. At noon the signal was given to prepare for battle and the whole force formed a line and, led by Stewart aboard the *Syren*, advanced to attack. The line comprised the *Constitution*, the brigs *Argus* and *Scourge*, the schooners *Vixen* and *Enterprise*, two mortar vessels, and six gunboats.

Within reach of the enemy's fire, the gunboats were cast off, and American sailors boarded the Tripolitan gunboats, twenty of which were moored in a line, outside the reef which forms the harbour. Three of these were seized and brought off under the cover of fire, and added to the American squadron.

Over the coming weeks Preble led further bombardments. In one escapade, he decided to send in the ***Intrepid*** at night, this time filled with explosives, in an attempt to destroy the Tripolitan fleet. Preble selected the men for this operation, and put Richard Somers in command of the thirteen chosen. Stephen Decatur's younger brother James was second in command. The plan was that, when the ketch was on course to collide with the fleet, Somers would start a series of fires on board and he and his crew would abandon ship. In the event, the explosives detonated prematurely and all thirteen were killed. (see map of Tripoli on page 22)

*The bombardment of Tripoli, showing from left to right, foreground: the **Enterprise**, **Nautilus**, **Argus**, **Syren**, **Vixen**, and **Constitution**.*

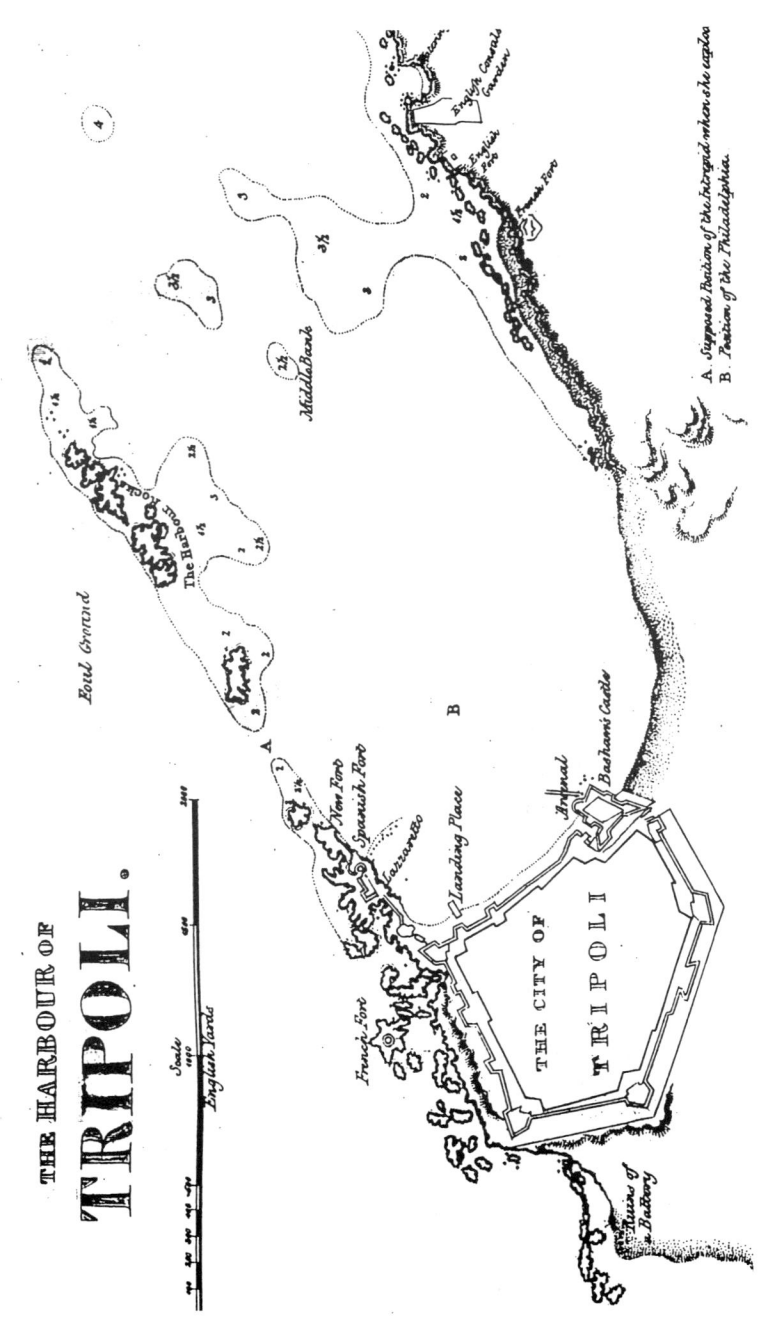

Old Map of Tripoli; published shortly after blockade

Three

Captain Charles Stewart

Stewart's gallantry in the siege of Tripoli won him promotion to the rank of master commandant and he was put in command of the frigate *Essex*. At the end of the fighting with Tripoli, he was ordered to take the *Essex* to Tunis.

At this time animosity towards the United States was mounting in Tunisia, fuelled by the hostile attitude of the squadron based there. It was so bad that George Davis, the Consul, had to take refuge on board the fleet. Relations were so strained that it was generally felt that it was only a matter of time before a state of war was declared.

The commander-in-chief, Commodore Rodgers, called an emergency meeting of those representing the parties concerned, and he explained the situation to all. Charles Stewart was elected to act as spokesman for the naval officers and, by diplomacy, he helped to negotiate a solution acceptable to all parties.

When this news reached President Jefferson, he expressed his "high satisfaction" at having an officer in the squadron who so thoroughly understood international law, the constitution of his country, and the policy of his government.

New York & Washington

After the "Tunisian affair", Stewart, now captain, was given command of the frigate *Constellation*. He returned to America, where he spent the years 1806-7 overseeing the construction of gunboats in New York. The next four years were spent mostly in protecting mercantile enterprises in the Mediterranean, the Adriatic, and the East Indies.

In 1811, American resentment was aroused by the activities of the Royal Navy in impressing U.S. seamen, blockading American ports, and enforcing the Orders in Council that barred neutral shipping from trading with French ports. They also objected to British support for Indian raids on American settlements.

President James Madison prohibited trade with Britain and in 1812 declared war in reaction to the overt acts Britain had taken against American commerce and its independent status.

At the time of the declaration of war Stewart and William Bainbridge went to Washington to seek service. They were informed by the Navy Department that it had been decided by the cabinet to place all the ships of war in the harbour at New York, for its defence.

They went to see President Madison at once and pleaded that "for the honour of the flag the United States Navy should be allowed to fight." Bainbridge claimed that their men were better, more disciplined, and that they fired cannon with as sure an aim as musketry, while the British fired at random.

There was further discussion before Madison asked, "You will give us victories, then, you think?" Stewart lost no time in saying, "We do, and not upon irrational premises."

"Bastards and Outlaws"

The persuasiveness of their arguments made Madison reconsider, and the next day he argued with his Cabinet before overruling it and decreeing that each Navy ship should be given one cruise before being laid up.

Commodore John Rodgers was dispatched with three heavy frigates and a sloop-of-war on 21 June 1812, his main objective being to intercept a big British convoy from the West Indies. He missed it and had to abandon the exercise when a gun on his flagship blew up.

This cruise seemed to confirm Washington's unfavourable opinion of the Navy, which was not that different from that expressed in *The Times* of London, that the Yankee fleet was "a handful of fir-built frigates manned by bastards and outlaws."

The day after Rodgers set sail, Stewart was appointed to the command of the brig *Argus* and the **Hornet** sloop-of-war.

In July, the brig **Nautilus** was captured by the British and, in a separate encounter, the **Constitution** may have fallen to them but for the skill of Captain Isaac Hull, in an epic chase of over 66 hours. There were also heavy defeats on land, at Fort Mackinac, Fort Dearborn (present-day Chicago), and Detroit.

It was not until the **Essex**, under David Porter, took the **Alert** on 13 August, that the Americans had their first real success of the war. Later that week, the **Constitution** engaged in battle with the **Guerriere**, and won.

After each victory, a celebratory ball was held in Washington. It was at one of these that the Navy Secretary, Paul Hamilton, proclaimed to one and all: "Never forget that it is to Captains Bainbridge and Stewart that you really owe these victories!"

*Men of the **Constitution** cheer as their ship goes into battle against the **Guerriere**.*

Again the Constellation

In December Stewart was appointed to the command of the frigate *Constellation*, then being repaired in Washington. When she was ready, he held a ball on board. Although he was the host - and by his reckoning the event cost him three years' salary - the idea for the ball had been Paul Hamilton's. He wished to win congressional sympathy for his naval expansion plans. President and Mrs Madison attended, along with some 600 dignitaries.

After this, Stewart once again went to war. Within days, while the *Constellation* was lying off the coast, Stewart saw enemy ships approaching: a superior force of two 74-gun men-of-war, three frigates, and several other vessels of war. He lost no time in retreating against such mighty opposition.

It being calm, he began kedging his frigate towards Norfolk, while the enemy fleet approached rapidly with a fine breeze until that dropped, and they were caught on the ebb tide, and were forced to anchor. Meanwhile, the *Constellation* had run aground on a sandbank, where she lay all that day.

Stewart had already begun to lighten his vessel and was even prepared - should the enemy get the benefit of a breeze and get within range - to burn

Charles Stewart; by Thomas Sully

his ship. However, the night flood saved him from such drastic measures and, with a fine breeze rising, boats with lights and pilots were sent to locate the shallows, and the *Constellation* was able to escape. She later took up a mooring between the forts of Norfolk and Nelson, where she contributed to their defence and repelled the British attack.

USS Constitution

In the summer of 1813, Captain Stewart was ordered to assume command of the frigate *Constitution*, then undergoing repairs in Boston. This was the command he had wanted, to be master of the warship designed to be the fastest and most powerful in the world, for her size.

One of the original six frigates ordered by George Washington, the *Constitution* entered service on 21 October 1797. She was equipped with 24-pound guns instead of the usual 18-pounders, and her decks were strengthened with enormous beams. Her sleek lines were based on those of the Baltimore clippers and the shape of the hull and the wider distance of the gun ports were so designed to give her the advantage in gunnery. In her refit in Boston she had been further improved, and now had a furnace for the provision of red-hot shot.

Although she was at this time over fifteen years old and had been in some mighty fights, most recently with the *Guerriere*, and the *Java*, the

*The final scene of the **Constitution** leaving the **Java**; her crew having been taken off, she was blown up.*

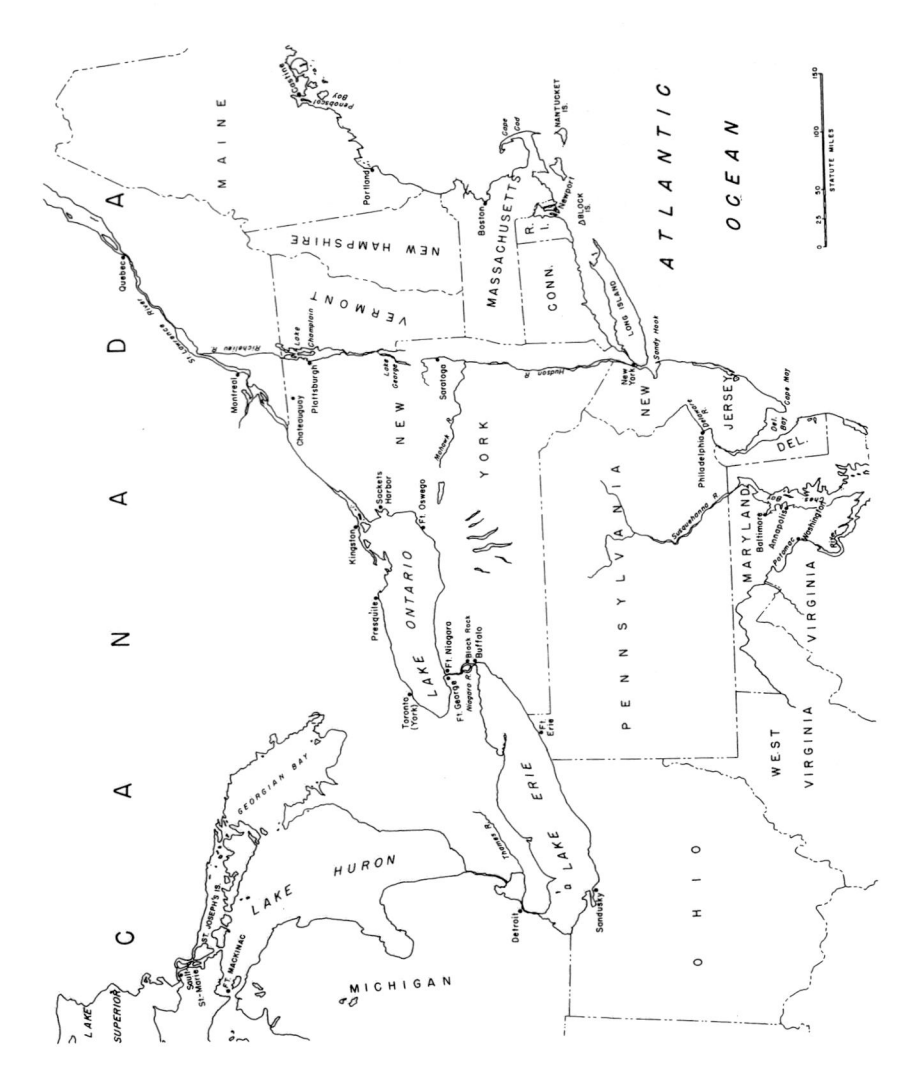

Map of the Eastern Seaboard, at the time of the 1812 War.

British still regarded the *Constitution* as the prize possession of the American fleet. It was during her battle with the *Guerriere*, when the shots she took were seen to make no impression on the *Constitution*'s solid oak planking that one sailor was heard to cry out that her sides were made of iron. It was from this that she gained the renown of her title - "Old Ironsides"!

Charles Stewart was honoured to be offered her command, particularly at such a crucial stage of the war. It was at this point in his life, at the age of thirty-five, that Stewart, already recognised as a great seaman and a captain of distinction, was preparing to set out on two separate voyages; one aboard the ship he had longed to master; the other in his forthcoming marriage to a daughter of a respected and influential family from Boston society, Delia Tudor.

Four

Delia Tudor & the Tudor Family

In the 16th Century, when the world was dominated by Portugal and Spain, with vast quantities of gold and silver coming from their colonies in America, the great wealth of these Catholic empires attracted the envy and enterprise of the Protestant countries of Europe. English, French, and Dutch adventurers began to challenge the Spanish claim to be "Lordes of halfe the World."

It was for more spiritual reasons that, on 16 September 1620, a group of pilgrims left Plymouth, England, on the *Mayflower*, their intended destination, Virginia. Bad navigation led them instead to Cape Cod, in Massachusetts. There they settled, and learned about American vegetables from the Indians. They shot turkeys and fished for clams and seemed content with the life they carved for themselves in the New World.

Ten years after they landed, the puritan lawyer John Winthrop arrived, with his "family" of five hundred men, women, and children. He had come with the purpose of creating a community where the religious beliefs of he and his followers could be practised freely. By integrating with the pilgrim settlers, he became the founding father of the Massachusetts Bay Colony.

In 1643 the Puritan colonies of Massachusetts, Connecticut, Plymouth and New Haven united to form the New England dominion, and within five years their trading with Spain, Madeira and the Canaries began to lift the colony out of economic depression.

The Coming of the Tudors

John Tudor was six years old when he arrived in the Massachusetts Bay Colony in 1715 with his mother. She was a widow who had braved the elements in search of a better life for herself and her only child. In time she remarried and provided him with the stability of a family; a stepfather and a half-sister.

Tudor's lack of formal education was compensated for by a sharp business acumen, and the desire to work hard. With his mother's help he began a small bakery, which proved so successful that he was, in a few years, able to progress and become a trader and general merchant. His speculative forays into the buying and selling of real estate were equally sound and he was soon well established in the community.

He married Jane Varney in 1732, and in time became a Deacon of the Congregational Church, becoming active in a civic capacity. Between the years 1751 and 1760 he was regularly elected as one of Boston's Overseers of the Poor. In 1763 he served as Surveyor of Wheat, a position he held for ten years.

His considerable wealth, and clerical and civic affiliations allowed him to establish himself in Boston society, as he found that colonials could scale such heights more rapidly than in Britain. He had one son, William, born in 1750, and he determined to give him the opportunities of education he had been denied, and duly sent him to Harvard.

By the time he died, in 1796, at the age of 85, John Tudor had seen his family become well connected, in business and society, the tentacles of the dynasty he had begun reaching out, even beyond America.

William Tudor

William Tudor graduated from Harvard at the age of 19 and was taken on immediately as a law clerk in the Boston offices of one of the most respected lawyers of his day, John Adams. Adams was destined to become the new Republic's first Vice President, before succeeding George Washington.

It would seem that Washington shared Adams' faith in the young man, for in 1776, at the age of only 26, William Tudor was appointed Judge Advocate General of the Continental Army.

With the rank of a colonel and the title of Judge, he oversaw courts martial; mutinies, desertions, and riots being frequent among the demoralised, ill-paid recruits. He developed a low opinion of the spirit of the colonial army and, in writing to his father in 1776, said that the Connecticut militia who had gone home in vast numbers when their year-long enlistment was up "had behaved disgracefully". He detested their "mercenary disposition" in demanding money to re-enlist.

He was, at the same time, bitter that others were growing rich in civilian life while he earned a contemptible army salary of under $50 a month. His own patriotism was not often tested in the heat of battle and, just before resigning from the post, in March 1777, he undertook the task of revising the Articles of War. One of these was the introduction of flogging in order to instil patriotism into a militia he despised. (By coincidence, just over one hundred years later, Tudor's great-grandson, Charles Stewart Parnell, would campaign successfully to have flogging abolished from the regulations of the British army.)

After the army, Tudor served as a member of the Massachusetts Legislature. In 1778 he married Delia Jarvis, the daughter of a prominent Boston family. They had six children: William Jr, born 1779; John, 1780; Frederic, 1783; Emma, 1785; Delia, 1787; and Henry, 1791. Two of his sons were destined to become famous in their own right.

William Tudor Jr

After Harvard and helping his brother Frederic establish his business, William Jr became a Member of the Massachusetts Legislature and established himself as a writer. As such he was a member of the Anthology Society, contributing to its magazine *Monthly Anthology and Boston Review*. He also founded the Boston Athenaeum, and was the first to suggest the purchase of land for the erection of the Bunker Hill Monument.

In 1815 he founded and became the first editor of the *North American Review*, was a member of the Massachusetts Historical Society, and published a criticism of contemporary manners in *Letters on the Eastern States*, in 1820. After this he wrote and published *The Life of James Otis*, in 1823, the same year in which he was appointed U.S. Consul in Peru. He was duly appointed Charge-d'affaires, in Rio de Janeiro, in 1827. He died of a rare tropical illness on 9 March 1830, aged 51.

Frederic Tudor

Of William and Delia's sons, three of them followed in their father's footsteps, in going to Harvard, but Frederic decided at an early age that his time would be better served in the practicality of inventing, and marketing his inventions.

Inspired by the taunts of his brothers as to why he did not break up the ice from the ponds of Boston and ship it to the tropics, he seized on a brainwave. He shipped one hundred and thirty tons of ice to Martinique, only to have it melt in six weeks.

After several abortive experiments he discovered that the most satisfactory form of insulation was sawdust, and that the ice needed to be in blocks of a uniform size. With the help of a friend he designed an ice cutter which had two parallel iron runners with saw teeth. This he dragged across the ponds of Boston and over the next fifteen years Frederic negotiated a deal with the authorities whereby he had title to all ponds in New England and he built a comprehensive supply network. He got monopoly rights on building ice houses in New Orleans and Charleston, from where his own fleet of modified ships carried thousands of tons of ice to Havana, the West Indies, Europe, Persia, and India.

Frederic Tudor may have been one of the first entrepreneurs to discover the golden rule of merchandising, that of creating a demand for something the customer did not know they wanted in the first place. He sailed halfway around the world convincing people that iced drinks were essential to a full and better life, that a hospital without ice was incomplete, and that ice cream after a meal was the only civilised way to eat. Shortly fashionable restaurants from London to Cairo were serving ice cream.

Frederic Tudor - "The Ice King" - is sometimes regarded as the archetypal American businessman and advertiser at their most charismatic.

So great was the attraction of running his business that he did not find time to marry until middle age, by which time his two older brothers had died, John in 1801, at the age of 21, and William in 1830; both unmarried.

In 1834 Frederic married Euphemia Fenno; at 19, a girl almost a third his age. They had six children and enjoyed thirty years together before he died in 1864 at the age of 80.

His sister Emma had married long before, in 1805, to Robert Hallowell Gardiner, a wealthy young aesthete, and they lived in the town of Gardiner, Maine, where he had inherited a large estate on the Kennebec River. There they lived in piety and peace, sharing their beloved literary pursuits with their nine children.

Delia Tudor

Delia was less fortunate than her brothers or sister in that by the time she became of age, her parents had made a life for themselves where self-indulgence came before any other consideration. When her father inherited $40,000 from old John Tudor, he quit his law practice and political life and went to France and England for a year, to enjoy himself.

In order to finance another trip, this time with his wife and daughter, William needed to mortgage his home. In Paris, where they were received at the court of Napoleon and Josephine, and later in London, they continued in that contentious vein, of spending their children's inheritance.

When they returned to Boston, they left young Delia in London, where she was to remain for the next five years, supported by money sent by her brother Frederic. She was an attractive and well-educated, intelligent woman, who, at the age of 26, was still single and, due to her parents' prodigality, was likely to remain so, with nothing visible on the horizon.

All that changed when she was forced to return to Boston at the outbreak of war, in June 1812, when, for the sake of expediency more than anything, she accepted the only suitor available; one of high rank, growing reputation, and considerable wealth. So it was that, in November 1813, Delia Tudor married Charles Stewart, Captain, United States Navy.

Delia Tudor Stewart, from an unfinished oil painting by Gilbert Stuart, circa 1815

Five

Stewart and the *USS Constitution*

In less than one week, in February 1814, Charles Stewart and the crew of the *Constitution* brought about the capture of the British merchant ship *Lovely Ann*, the schooner *Phoenix*, as well as destroying the schooner *Picton*, and the brig *Catherine*, all in the waters off the coast of Guyana.

Within days she was to chase the frigate *La Pique* and several other British warships, in the Mona passage off Puerto Rico. Stewart was unable to overtake any because of the poor state of the sails on the *Constitution*. (With good sails and conditions, the *Constitution* was capable of a top speed of 13.5 knots.)

There had been a time not so long before, when a ship the size of the 36-gun *La Pique* would have taken on the *Constitution*, eager to fight, but the results of some of these attacks had shaken such "uncircumspect gallantry" out of the British Admiralty if not out of the British commanders too. Her captain had written instructions not to engage a ship of that weight.

However, Stewart decided to return home and replace his sails, and on the morning of 3 April, while heading for Portsmouth, the wind shifted to the northeast, and he decided to make for Boston. But when the wind dropped and the *Constitution* lay in calm waters about three miles southeast of Thatcher's Island, two square-riggers were seen to windward. These were British men-of-war; the *Junon*, and the *Tenedos*, both with 50 guns.

*The **Constitution** escapes from the **Tenedos** and the **Junon**; from an old wood-cut.*

A Lightened Ship

As Stewart had no pilot aboard, he did not dare to risk taking the channel between Baker's Island and the Misery and running for Salem, so he set for Halfway Rock, keeping in deep water. Meanwhile he lightened ship by throwing overboard spare spars, provisions, and booty, and pumping out. One account of the day claims that only when the whiskey in the spirit-room had been pumped overboard did the **Constitution** reach her proper level, and begin to draw ahead of her pursuers.

By noon, the **Constitution** rounded Halfway Rock and made for Marblehead, and within the hour was anchored under the guns of Fort Sewall, the **Junon** and the **Tenedos** lying six miles off. Fearing the frigates would pursue and attack the **Constitution**, a number of measures were taken to lend assistance; guns were sent from Salem; the Marblehead artillery battalion were put under arms; Commodore Bainbridge sent men from the Charlestown Navy Yard, and the New England Guards started to march from Boston. But none of these resources proved necessary, as the British, after a while, sailed away.

The Blockade of Boston

Three days later the **Constitution** hurried in to Boston Harbour where she was to remain for eight and a half months, blockaded by the British.

During that time there were constant reports that Boston was to be the subject of a combined land and sea attack and Bostonians voiced their concern that the presence of ships in the harbour was more likely to attract enemy fire. The ***Constitution*** was anchored so as to cover the entrance to the harbour and the unfinished ***Independence*** was moored up with a few guns hastily mounted.

The speed with which the British were able to blockade Boston made it clear that their ships were travelling in company. In no time the blockade spread to other ports and presently they were joined by the impressive ship of the line ***HMS Ramillies***, under Rear Admiral Thomas Hardy, the man famous for the part he played in Lord Nelson's victory at Trafalgar in 1805.

Like the Eastern seaports, New Orleans had also become a focus of attention, as the early elements of a British amphibious expedition that included 7,500 troops under Major General Sir Edward Pakenham anchored at the mouth of the Mississippi. They began to advance on New Orleans, where General Andrew Jackson had already begun to prepare his fortifications.

Peace talks had begun in Ghent in August 1814, and now while most Americans anxiously awaited word either from there or from New Orleans, their warships still put to sea if they could. As the knot tightened around the area from Cape Cod to Cape Ann, Stewart became more and more frustrated. Day after day, and night after night he waited, biding his time, waiting for the optimum moment. It came when the British despatched three of their fleet to Halifax for stores. On 14 December, Charles Stewart, aboard the ***Constitution***, took advantage of a westerly gale and slipped out of Boston.

Within days he scuttled the brig ***Lord Nelson***, east of Bermuda, and four days after this victory, on 28 December, the Treaty of Ghent was ratified by the Prince Regent and dispatched to President Madison in Washington. However, hostilities were to continue for some time and, on 8 January 1815, Pakenham began his offensive against the troops of General Jackson.

On 16 February the ***Constitution*** captured the merchant ship ***Susannah***, off Lisbon, and the following day the United States ratified the Treaty of Ghent, thus ending the war.

*The **Constitution** as depicted on a commemorative metal tray issued for the American Bicentennial, in 1976.*

Six

His Greatest Victory

On the night of 19 February 1815, a group of lieutenants stood on the quarterdeck of the *Constitution* talking about the fact that they had not met a ship of equal force during the cruise, when they were joined by Captain Stewart, who had overheard their conversation.

Unaware that a treaty had been agreed, he assured the men that "before the sun again rises and sets, you will be engaged in battle with the enemy, and it will not be with a single ship."

Stewart was a man given to making predictions; he believed in them, and although in this case he anticipated combat he could not have foreseen that it was to provide him with his greatest victory, or that the *Constitution* "would achieve her greatest triumph and perform her most brilliant service."

The Chance Offered

By noon the next day the *Constitution* was within 180 miles of Madeira, a light easterly breeze drifting over the water, and the sky cloudy, when at one o'clock in the afternoon, a sail was seen a little on the port bow. Hauling the *Constitution* up to the point, Stewart gave chase, and an hour later a second sail appeared beyond the first.

By this time the first ship's hull was above the horizon, and because of false ports painted on her side she had the look of a fifty-gun ship. When this was suggested by a lieutenant to him, Stewart replied: "Be this as it may, you know I promised you a fight before the setting of today's sun, and if we do not take it now that it is offered, we can scarcely have another chance. We must flog them when we catch them, whether she has one gun-deck or two!"

The ships in question were British: the 20-gun frigate **Cyane**, under Captain Thomas Gordon Falcon, and the 18-gun sloop-of-war **Levant**, under Captain the Honourable George Douglass. They were part of the British squadron cruising the area.

The Chance Taken

While under blockade on the **Constellation** or while bottled up in Boston Harbour on the **Constitution**, Stewart must have long since abandoned hopes for glory in this war.

And so, unaware that the signatures of emissaries many miles away had effectively put paid to that opportunity, he gave the command to open fire, and the ships began trading shots under a clear moon.

So skilful and threatening were the thrusts of his lightweight adversaries, that Stewart's advantage of long 24-pounders may have been considerably lessened but for the benefit of his natural seamanship.

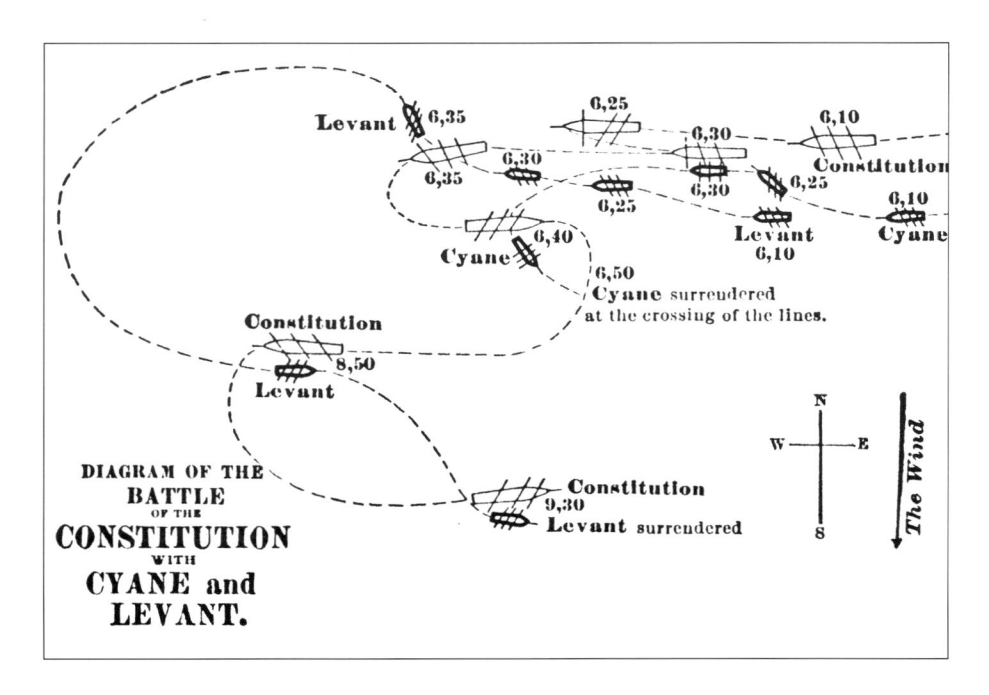

DIAGRAM OF THE BATTLE OF THE CONSTITUTION WITH CYANE and LEVANT.

The Tales They Do Tell . . .

Like the myriad of marine life proliferating beneath the sea, antiquarian books of sea yarns and shanties are packed with the stuff of great victories. And in the case of the **Constitution**'s finest fight one eyewitness account tells how, after an initial exchange of shots and a chase, the **Cyane** and the **Levant** formed in line, their sails full, awaiting the **Constitution** ...

"Then she came, ploughing down with the wind over her port quarter. As she arrived opposite the two ships she stripped off her canvas, as a fighter his shirt, and wearing around she ranged up on the starboard tack to windward of the two Britishers, and at 6.10 o'clock, with the **Cyane** three hundred yards away on the port bow, opened fire on both."

As the smoke cleared, the **Levant** could be seen ahead of the **Cyane**, out of the range of the **Constitution**, and she began to turn, preparing to rake her. Stewart had guessed her strategy and, as she sailed up to cross his bows, he filled the sails of the **Constitution**, put his helm up, bluffed the **Cyane** down to leeward, and, going forward, crossed under the **Levant**'s stern, pouring in two raking broadsides in swift succession.

The **Levant** had had enough and sped away, to take stock of her damage. At the same time the **Cyane** tried to escape but Stewart crossed her stern from starboard to port and raked her. She managed to get off one shot, but it bounced off the bows of the **Constitution** and, forty minutes after fighting began, the **Cyane** struck her colours.

*The **Constitution** captures the **Levant** and the **Cyane**.*

Two hours later the *Levant* returned to find out the situation and as soon as it was seen that the *Cyane* had surrendered she exchanged broadsides with the *Constitution* and went to escape. The *Constitution* gave chase and fired shot after shot at her until the *Levant* also struck her colours.

Another story from the day tells of how John Lancey, a sailor who, as the battle against the *Levant* went on, lay dying. When the surgeon told him that death was nigh, he replied: "I only want to hear that the other has struck." Later, as a big cheer went up, Lancey raised his head, waved an arm that had been partly shot away, gave three feeble cheers, and fell back dead.

"A Right Good Song"

The victory was commemorated in many ways, in oils, in gold, and in ink, but none is more rousing than the lyrics of what is described as "a right good song" of the time:

> Then a lifting rift in the mist showed up
>   The stout *Cyane* close-hauled
> To swing in our wake and our quarter rake,
>   And a boasting Briton bawled:
>
> "Starboard or larboard we've got him fast
>   Where his heels won't take him through;
> Let him luff or wear, he'll find us there -
>   Ho, Yankee! Which will you do?"
>
> We did not luff and we did not wear,
>   But braced our top-sails back,
> Till the sternway drew in fair and true
>   Broadsides athwart her track.
>
> Athwart her track and across her bows
>   We raked her fore and aft,
> And out of the fight and into the night
>   Drifted the beaten craft.

Seven

The Aftermath

As soon as both ships had been boarded by his lieutenants, the victorious Stewart invited the British commanders to his cabin where, over a fraternal dram, they amicably discussed the fine points of seamanship involved in the battle. There was no sign of personal animosity towards his "gallant foes".

Another tale recounts how at this time a midshipman came into Stewart's cabin to ask if the crew were to have their evening grog. As the time for serving it had passed before the battle began, Stewart expressed surprise, thinking they had imbibed. The midshipman explained that it had been ready, but that the men had not wanted "Dutch courage" and the grog-tub had been capsized in the lee scuppers. Stewart gave his assent.

Later, when an argument flared up between the British captains, each blaming the other for making manoeuvres that had lost the battle, Stewart intervened. "Gentlemen," he said, "there is no use getting warm about it; it would have been the same whatever you might have done. If you doubt that, I will put you all on board again and you can try it over."

This may have been an obscure reference to his presentiment of the previous night, or he may have been heady with his success. As an officer who had stood alongside Barry and Preble, Stewart knew that his was a splendid feat of seamanship.

"Brilliant Naval Battle"

This was regarded as one of the most brilliant naval battles on record, for the size of the enemy force engaged. The skill demonstrated by Stewart in handling his ship against two brave and resourceful antagonists has perhaps never been excelled.

	Comparative Force			
	Guns	Metal	Crew	Loss
Constitution	54	684	456	15
Cyane & *Levant*	55	763	320	77

In naval battles of this period, where one ship was engaging two, it was most unusual for the single ship to avoid being raked by one or other of her antagonists. The **Constitution** was not raked once in this fight. On the contrary, she repeatedly raked both of her antagonists, backing and filling in the smoke of battle, and forcing the British ships down to leeward in an exceptional series of manoeuvres.

Three years before, in February 1812, a French 44-gun frigate separately engaged the British **Rainbow**, 26 guns, and **Avon**, 18, and after a long battle all three of the combatants separated, and both French and British stated the other fled; however, Stewart had fought his opponents together, and captured both.

Escape from St Jago

The task completed, Stewart proceeded to the island of St Jago intending to unload his cargo of more than 300 prisoners! While negotiating for their disembarkation at Porto Praya, the British squadron reached the **Constitution** in thick fog. Under the command of Sir George Collier, the squadron consisted of the **Newcastle**, 64 guns, **Leander**, 64, and **Acasta**, 50.

Stewart had to escape in a hurry, and gave orders to cut the cables and crowd sails. Although it was a neutral port, the Americans knew that the British had recently disregarded such protocol at Fayal, in the Azores, and at Valparaiso. Within ten minutes from when the first ship was seen, the **Constitution** and her prizes were sailing out of the harbour together.

As the American ships slipped through the fog the guns in the battery on shore began to boom. A number of prisoners from the captured British ships had been left behind in the chaos of the evacuation, and were now firing to attract the attention of the squadron, but the British ships were coming from the south, up against a stiff northeasterly breeze. The ***Constitution*** and her prizes hugged the east side of the port and got out to windward of the enemy.

Until clear of the harbour, the Americans sailed under nothing higher than their topsails, thereby escaping the lookouts. But once clear, the topgallant sail and royal-yards were crossed and the sails instantly spread to the breeze. At this point the Americans were only a mile or so to windward of the British.

The Chase at Sea

The ***Constitution***'s log notes that at 12.50 she was holding her own with the ***Newcastle*** and the ***Leander*** on her leeward quarter, while the ***Acasta***, astern, was dropping out of the race. The log of the ***Acasta*** says that while the ***Constitution*** was getting away from her, she in turn was gaining on her two prizes.

At 1.10 Stewart ordered Lieutenant Hoffman, on the ***Cyane***, to tack - change direction by passing the bow of the ship through the eye of the wind. Before this the ***Cyane*** had been rapidly dropping into the hands of the British. Once Hoffman obeyed, she sailed away and escaped altogether, the three pursuers content to close on the ***Constitution*** and the ***Levant***.

Thirty five minutes later, the ***Newcastle*** opened fire on the ***Constitution***, the two ships being so close that the officers, standing on the hammock-nettings, could see each other clearly. The shots fell short and the chase continued for well over an hour. At three o'clock, when Stewart became concerned about the lagging ***Levant***, he signalled her to tack, as he had the ***Cyane***.

On board the ***Levant***, Lieutenant Ballard did as instructed and, to his surprise, and, indeed, to Stewart's, all three British ships tacked after her, and the ***Constitution*** sailed away free.

The Levant Recaptured

The three frigates chased the ***Levant*** all the way back to the port of St Jago, where, with the assistance of the escaped prisoners who were still manning the cannons there, they fired broadside after broadside at the sloop.

They continued their bombardment for fifteen minutes without a single shot striking her hull. Finally, Lieutenant Ballard hauled down his flag.

After his escape, Captain Stewart took the **Constitution** to Sao Luís, in Brazil, and landed the prisoners, refreshed his crew, and refitted his vessel. He then returned to Boston, where he and his men were welcomed home with great celebrations. (In the meantime, the **Cyane** had reached New York on 10 April.)

The Captain's Account

U.S. Frigate Constitution, May --, 1815.

Sir,

On the 20th of February last, the island of Madeira bearing about west south-west, distant 60 leagues, we fell in with his Britannic majesty's two ships of war, the Cyane and Levant; and brought them to action about 6 o'clock in the evening, both of which, after a spirited engagement of 40 minutes, surrendered to the ship under my command.

Considering the advantages derived by the enemy, from a divided and more active force, as also their superiority in the weight and number of guns, I deem the speedy and decisive result of this action the strongest assurance which can be given to the government, that all under my command did their duty, and gallantly supported the reputation of American seamen.

Enclosed you will receive the minutes of the action(*), and a list of the killed and wounded on board this ship; also enclosed you will receive for your information, a statement of the actual force of the enemy, and the number killed and wounded on board their ships, as near as could be ascertained.

I have the honour to be, &c.

Charles Stewart

Hon. Secretary of the Navy.

American loss - 3 killed, 12 wounded.
British loss - 35 killed, 42 wounded.
Prisoners taken, 313.   *(*):(see Appendix)*

48

Honour Upon Honour

Later, in New York, the council honoured Captain Stewart with the freedom of their city, and threw a public dinner for him and his officers. On arrival in Philadelphia, he was received by the legislature of his native State, who voted him their thanks. The governor presented him with a gold-hilted sword, in recognition of his capture of the two ships.

In Washington, the assembled Congress resolved that a suitable gold medal should be presented to Stewart, his officers, and crew in commemoration of their victory.

*The medal awarded to Charles Stewart after his battle with the **Cyane** and the **Levant**.*

When the British Admiralty held a court of inquiry into the incident, the captains of the *Newcastle* and *Leander* both stated that they thought the 18-gun *Levant*, described as "a manifestly smaller ship", to be one of the American vessels: **President,** 44 guns, **Congress,** 36, or **Macedonian,** 38. It may have been that the commanders were just taking the Admiralty's instructions to avoid "uncircumspect gallantry" literally. However, ten years later, Sir George Collier, the squadron's commander, committed suicide after his failure was thrown in his face at a public meeting.

The End of the 1812 War

The last naval action of the war took place on 30 June 1815, four months after the ratification of the treaty. In spite of the fact that the United States

Navy had borne serious losses it emerged from an ill-advised war a strong and capable force whose losses had been offset by captures. The American power at sea and their excellent gunnery came as a shock to Britain, bringing the loss of over 1600 merchant ships.

Although later naval historians have overlooked the relevance of Stewart's victory, in America at that time its effect was that it was an important propaganda victory for a young country which had suffered some humiliating military defeats. Stewart's victory was the perfect morale-boosting fillip.

Eight

After the Glory

After the war, Stewart bought "Montpelier", a 225-acre estate in New Jersey. Overlooking the Delaware river, it stood between the townships of Bordentown and Fieldsboro, and cost $16,000.

Of the two houses on the estate, he had the larger, which was built in 1797 by Francois Frederici, the "General of Surinam", remodelled in the federal style. He added a second floor and, beneath its hipped roof, built a pillared terrace at the front. In the grounds he planted silver birch, to protect the house from the wind that came down the river valley, and he turned his mind to more peaceful, agricultural, interests when he was not away at sea. His role in being the captain of "Old Ironsides" at the height of the war had the effect of linking her sobriquet with him, so that it became synonymous with him. Eventually his rural estate also became known as "Ironsides".

A Point in "Persuasion"

Although Delia Stewart lived at "Ironsides" for several years, the indications are that she was not happy there. For the society belle who had enjoyed London and Paris for so long, life on a rural estate in New Jersey may not have measured up to her aspirations. She was an educated woman who could read Latin and Greek, was fluent in French, Spanish, Italian, and German, and enjoyed the company of people of culture. Although she knew before her marriage that Stewart was devoid of certain social graces, she had perhaps hoped, in time, to broaden his horizons beyond his preferred company, that of fellow seafarers.

The house on the Montpelier estate where Charles Stewart lived for over fifty years.

Perhaps she could empathise with Jane Austen's obnoxious Sir Walter Elliot, who, on seeing an admiral he knew, believed he had never seen quite so wretched an example of what seafaring could do to a man, generalising unmercifully in his view that "they are all knocked about, and exposed to every climate, and every weather, till they are not fit to be seen."

Stewart had been exposed to such elements for almost a quarter of a century, and the saltiness of this weatherbeaten image in her drawing room may not have been as aesthetically pleasing as Delia had first imagined.

Delia may also have concurred with Sir Walter on another point, that "a man is in greater danger in the navy of being insulted by the rise of one whose father, his father might have disdained to speak to . . ." There can be little doubt that her father, William, who could claim kinship to the Tudor dynasty, would most likely not have passed the time of day with Charles Stewart Sr.

USS Franklin

So it was that after the ringing endorsements of his splendid seamanship lulled a little, the captain and his lady found time to sample domesticity together. Their first baby, William, died in infancy, and in 1816, their daughter Delia Tudor Stewart was born.

In 1817, Stewart was promoted to the rank of commodore and the 74-gun ship of the line *Franklin* was to be his flagship. He was given command of the American squadron in the Mediterranean, and he left "Ironsides" in his wife's capable hands and went off to join his ship, then being fitted out at Philadelphia. The following year, while he was serving in the Mediterranean, his son Charles Tudor Stewart was born.

Returning from a tour of the Mediterranean in May 1821, Stewart met up with his old ally in victory and glory, the *Constitution*. The ship, now under the captaincy of Jacob Jones, was sailing for Gibraltar, to become the flagship of the Mediterranean squadron.

An Unrewarding Return

Once, when returning home after a two-year absence, Stewart found that Delia had sold off much of their livestock and furniture. She explained that she had been forced into this in order to pay off creditors, claiming that Stewart had not left her sufficient allowance to maintain the family and the estate.

If he was not already aware of his wife's approach to meeting the demands of necessity, this proved to be a rude and costly awakening. Although he had accepted her without a dowry, he must have realised at once that the one thing Delia Tudor did bring from her parents was their belief that survival always outstripped sentimentality.

In a letter Delia once wrote to her sister Emma, she said that she and Stewart had argued on their wedding night. His return to this situation must have overshadowed the pleasure of his homecoming and caused many more heated exchanges.

However, they overcame such squalls and, when Stewart was assigned to the squadron in the Pacific, Delia was pleased to go with him to see what life was like in the "South American Provinces". It would seem that she preferred it, for when the Admiral took up the post permanently in Lima, both she and the children went with him.

In July 1821, Peru had boldly declared itself independent of Spain and, although it was a time of high tension in the colony, Delia found the experience edifying and communicated this to her sister, saying that it made her the happiest she had been since getting married. It also gave her the chance to be of use, socially and intellectually, as she helped Stewart, by writing letters and frequently acting as his interpreter.

"A Spanish Gentleman"

For a few years things went well, before an incident occurred which was to change their lives completely. It happened when Delia was approached by a Spanish gentleman who came to her with letters of introduction from two of her friends. His story was that he needed to leave the country, and he was seeking her help to smuggle him out. There can be no doubt that Delia was aware of all the dangers inherent in so outrageous a request.

At this time the United States was treading a diplomatic path very cautiously in the war between Spain and her South American colony. How Delia reached the decision to help the Spaniard is now a matter for speculation, particularly in view of the fact that her elder brother, William, had been appointed U.S. Consul to Peru, taking up his post in Lima in 1823.

Whether, as was later suggested, she was involved in some sort of dalliance with the Spaniard, she never fully explained. She may have done it for altruistic reasons, or for excitement, or notoriety. She may have been duped, but she certainly left herself open to blackmail.

Whichever it was, she took the decision to abuse her husband's position and place his reputation in jeopardy. In liaison with a ship's officer, she smuggled the Spanish gentleman on board the ***Franklin***, without Stewart's knowledge. It was only a matter of time before the Spaniard was discovered on the ship, and was exposed as a spy.

Court Martial

When the matter came to light, the Peruvian authorities lost no time in demanding a full explanation. The whole affair received a blaze of publicity and Stewart was recalled to Washington, to account for the episode and to be tried before a court martial.

Commodore Charles Stewart

In view of the fact that the United States was trying to remain neutral, a court martial was an inevitable consequence of such conduct. However, its prosecution was not without controversy at home; Andrew Jackson being vehemently opposed to it.

Delia caused Stewart further embarrassment when she chose not to accompany him to Washington, or to testify on his behalf, arguing that his excellent reputation would help him overcome the charges.

When the Stewarts returned to the United States, newspapers were carrying stories of how Delia had accepted a bribe of $30,000, and that she was in love with the Spanish spy. For his part, Stewart was subjected to a degrading arrest and, for the best part of a year, had the prospect of a trial hanging over him.

Paul Hamilton, his champion of old, had long since ceased to be Secretary of the Navy. Two other Secretaries had come and gone since then, and neither was held in high regard. Samuel Lewis Southard had become Secretary in September 1823 and he was a man who had very strict views on discipline, and lost little time in subjecting two heroes of the War of 1812 to a court martial.

Degradation of a Hero

The second man was Commodore David Porter, whose Pacific tour in the *Essex* had all but annihilated the British whaling industry. Southard incurred the undying wrath and enmity of Andrew Jackson by bringing both of these officers to trial.

Both cases were heard in 1825, by the same court martial board, Commodore James Barron being appointed president of the board. Barron had not commanded a naval vessel since 1807, when he was involved in the infamous Chesapeake-Leopard affair. And more recently, in 1820, he had killed Stewart's old friend Stephen Decatur in a duel. The explanation for his appointment was simple: Southard had recalled the officers who were available, and of these Barron was the senior.

The events which became known as the Chesapeake-Leopard Affair happened on 22 June 1807, when the **USS Chesapeake** was taking Barron to assume command in the Mediterranean. Intercepted by the British frigate **Leopard**, Barron refused to allow the British to board and search for deserters. Without any warning, the ***Leopard*** opened fire, catching the Americans unready. After 15 minutes of confusion, during which time an officer saved the ship's honour by carrying a burning coal from the galley to fire a single gun in her defence, Barron struck his colours.

Four of the ***Chesapeake***'s company were killed, and twenty, including Barron, wounded. A boarding party seized four men suspected of desertion, eventually hanging one, the only Briton of the four.

Barron was court-martialled. Stephen Decatur requested to be excused from sitting on the court martial because he and Barron had been close friends. His request was denied. Barron was found guilty of not clearing for action before the attack and was suspended from the navy for five years, whereupon he joined the merchant service.

Stranded in Europe at the outbreak of the 1812 War, Barron did not return home to reenter the navy until the end of the conflict. Although he claimed that he had been unable to get a passage earlier, many attributed his absence to cowardice. Hearing that Decatur was of this opinion, he challenged him, hoping to show his courage. A duel was arranged for a morning in March 1820, at Bladensburg, Maryland.

They almost reconciled their differences before the duel and, had their seconds intervened, the quarrel may have been resolved without bloodshed. As it was, neither shot to kill, Barron being hit in the thigh, Decatur in the hip by a ball that ricocheted up into his groin. He died after 12 hours of extreme agony. Barron recovered and in time became the most senior officer in the navy, even though he never again commanded at sea.

The Charges

On 18 August 1825 Stewart faced charges of misconduct; charges of "unofficerlike conduct, disobedience of orders, neglect of duty, and oppression and cruelty." The most important of the charges was the first. Specifically, Stewart was accused of building and operating vessels for his own account, carrying specie for American merchants for his own gain, transporting horses to Peru and selling them to the Spanish forces besieged there, and generally showing undue partiality to the Spanish.

The third charge, neglect of duty, concerned the infrequency of target practice on board the ***Franklin***; the last, oppression and cruelty, dealt with the alleged mistreatment of an officer who had been confined in the flagship while awaiting trial by court martial.

"The Highest Distinction"

Delia spent the summer of 1825 with her children on her brother Frederic's estate, at Nahant, north of Boston. Stewart was left to fend for himself, and she did not respond to his letters pleading with her to testify. She was finally persuaded to give her version of events, doing so in a notarised statement.

Following Stewart's passionately dramatic rebuttals, the court gave him "an acquittal, more honourable than the records of any naval tribunal can furnish". Twelve officers, "distinguished for their patriotism, valour, experience, and fidelity to their country", considered that Stewart had acted with "the highest distinction" in his duties.

Stewart's court martial was not a "whitewash" or its outcome a foregone conclusion. Southard was not simply going through the motions of humiliating him in public over Delia's indiscretion. Certainly Stewart never saw it as just a face-saving exercise; his anguished letters to Delia give some indication of this.

Further proof that the trials were not public-relations exercises can be seen in the outcome of the other court martial, of David Porter. He was tried for his handling of what had become known as the "Foxhardo" Affair.

This happened when two officers from the U.S. schooner ***Beagle*** landed at Fajardo, Puerto Rico, to investigate acts of piracy. The Spanish authorities chose to disbelieve the purpose of the visit and threw the men in gaol overnight. Angered by this, Porter went ashore with 200 seamen and demanded an apology to the officers, threatening the "total destruction of Foxhardo", if not. He got the apology, but, upon his return home, was berated for exceeding his instructions.

The court martial found him guilty and he was suspended for six months. Outraged again, he resigned, after 28 years' exemplary service, and accepted the appointment of Commander-in-chief of the Mexican Navy.

"More Frightful than the Loss of Life"

After his trial, Stewart returned to Philadelphia, where his old friends greeted him and gave a public dinner in his honour. Ostensibly this was for his services while in command in the Pacific, but in all probability it was to show their support for him after the ordeal of the past year.

Although Delia had finally given a statement, Stewart could not forgive her for her reluctance to testify personally. He found her attitude to a situation she had created, then exacerbated, totally unacceptable, as it nearly cost him his rank, something which he described later as "a calamity more frightful than the loss of life".

When she returned to Bordentown some five months later, it was to find that Stewart had left orders for her to be turned out of the house.

This was effectively the end of their marriage, although the acrimony of their separation would drag on for many years. He would never see or speak to her again and he refused to answer her pleading letters.

Nine

The Stewarts and the Parnells

Once the trial was over, Stewart returned to service, becoming involved in the examination of midshipmen, and serving on many court martial boards. At the same time he began a bitter fight for the control of his daughter and son.

His fear of public scandal restrained him from exercising his legal claim to his children too aggressively. Delia, however, afraid that he might attempt to remove the children forcibly, sent them to live with her sister, Emma, in Maine, for about a year while she agreed a settlement with Stewart.

It was three years after the end of the court martial before they reached a settlement agreeable to them both. She retained control of her daughter, but had to surrender her son to the care of his father. Each had access to the other child. The accumulated debts of the past three years were met by Stewart, in addition to which he gave his wife an annual income of $800, with another $600 for his daughter. Delia also retained her own and her children's right of inheritance to Stewart's property.

After all the drama and trauma of recent years, a return to "Ironsides", and its less demanding distractions, was all that Stewart sought. He adapted to the changes in his life, occupying himself with running the estate and indulging his interest in agriculture. He became better acquainted with his neighbours in Bordentown and Fieldsboro and, in time, found consolation in the company of a Mrs Field, a "pretty young married countrywoman".

In August 1830, the Admiral was appointed to the Board of Navy Commissioners in Washington. He remained on the board for three years, before retiring, to live on his farm. (This was not to last; he seemed to be incapable of separating himself for too long from the service of the navy.)

Mrs Field was now his constant companion and he referred to her as "Mrs Stewart", and treated her son, Robert, as his stepson. They could not marry, as he and Delia were not divorced, but she bore him a son, who, along with Robert Field, was to form a strong and lasting friendship with his legitimate son, Charles Tudor Stewart.

After attending a boarding school near Baltimore, Charles Tudor Stewart trained as an engineer and studied law. As a young man he worked on the Reading Railway. Despite having a deep affection for his mother and sister, he enjoyed a good relationship with Mrs Field, and her son.

While living in Bordentown, Charles also befriended Prince Lucien Murat, whose parents, Prince Joachim Murat and Caroline, sister of Napoleon I, had for a time settled on an estate close to "Ironsides". This was Point Breeze, a splendid mansion built by Napoleon's brother Joseph, when he had fled France after Waterloo. Charles established a friendship with Prince Lucien which, in later years, was to make him a very wealthy man.

The Marriage of Delia Tudor Stewart

After a number of years of living in boarding houses, Delia Stewart rented a small house in Washington with her mother, and her daughter. The younger Delia had grown into a "handsome and vivacious girl, with dark hair and blue eyes, an unusually oval face and pale complexion". She was by now attracting the attentions of several likely suitors. When a wealthy colonel named Philip White sought her hand her grandmother was in favour of the match, but Delia rejected his proposal. Within the year she became far more interested in the handsome John Henry Parnell.

Parnell was a 22-year-old Anglo-Irish landowner who was doing the "Grand Tour" with his cousin Lord Powerscourt, in the accepted social expedient of offering pedigree in exchange for more readily available wealth. He was the son of the late William Parnell, an M.P. and writer, whose works displayed a great social conscience over the plight of the poor in general, and of the underprivileged Catholics of Ireland in particular.

In May 1835, having met the young Delia on several occasions, John Henry Parnell wrote a letter to Admiral Stewart:

Sir,

I feel some hesitation, least you should think it presumption in me an entire stranger thus abruptly writing to you upon so delicate a subject, but I should consider that I did not do myself justice, if I delayed any longer communicating to you my feelings and wishes.

I met your daughter Miss Stewart here for the first time about twelve months since, and was very much struck with her, we subsequently met at West Point, Boston, and here again last winter. On leaving this to accompany Lord Powerscourt to Mexico, it was with the intention of returning in the spring, and I now flatter myself that I shall have no difficulty in obtaining her own and her mother's consent to our union, and only wait your favourable answer, when I shall forthwith do myself the pleasure of waiting upon you and shall be happy to give any explanations you may require.

I have the honour to remain,

Sir, yours respectfully,

J. Parnell

The Admiral, fearing that the young man might be nothing better than an adventurer, made strenuous enquiries about him before replying. He would not have needed to delve too deeply before learning that Parnell was from a family of the Ascendancy that was long established in Ireland.

In fact it was at the time of the Restoration of the Monarchy in Britain, that Thomas Parnell, a former mayor of Congleton, Cheshire, made the decision to live in Ireland. A man of considerable wealth, he bought a house in Dublin and an estate called Rathleague in Queen's County. His elder son, Thomas, became the Archdeacon of Clogher and a recognised poet, while his younger son, John, became a barrister, judge, and M.P.

John Parnell's daughter Anne married one, John Hayes, and their son, Samuel - M.P. for Wicklow (1783-90) - owned a home in Dublin and several farms in Wicklow until 1770, when he began to build a house in the Palladian style near Rathdrum. This was Avondale, and it duly passed into the Parnell family upon his death, in 1795.

It passed first to Sir John Parnell, Chancellor of the Irish Exchequer, then to one of his sons, William, before coming to his son, John Henry.

When Admiral Stewart satisfied himself that the young man was genuine, he duly gave the union his blessing. Plans went ahead for a wedding later that month, but they nearly went awry, when Stewart would not agree to increase his estranged wife's allowance, so that she could go and visit her daughter when she moved to Ireland. It was only when he saw that his intransigence was presenting a likely obstacle that he overcame his strong sense of grievance and promised to pay Delia her quarterly allowance in advance whenever she wanted to visit her daughter.

John Henry Parnell married Delia Tudor Stewart, at Grace Church, New York, on 31 May 1835. The couple then spent a few days at "Ironsides", and on 10 June were seen off from Charleston by the Admiral and his son on their voyage to London, and on to Avondale, County Wicklow.

Avondale, the Parnell residence in Wicklow.

Ten

Admiral Stewart's Legacy

In July 1836, Admiral Stewart was back in service; appointed a commissioner to prepare plans for the improvement of the Navy yard at Pensacola. On 1 July 1837, he replaced Commodore James Barron as commander of the Navy yard in Philadelphia.

The following year, on the strength of his great celebrity, he was persuaded to let his name be put forward as the Democratic candidate for the American presidency. Stewart supplied large sums to his campaign managers to buy up newspaper editors (the custom at the time) and "Old Ironsides" clubs were formed to promote his candidacy. Charles Tudor Stewart helped his father to run his campaign, by acting as his private secretary and closest advisor, but despite their best efforts, and the support of many senior Democrats who saw the Admiral's potential, they were unsuccessful in securing the nomination.

Although Jefferson had once complimented him on his grasp of the law and politics, Admiral Stewart at 60 was up against James Polk, a career politician and 17 years his junior. It does not seem to have been a very evenly matched contest, and, Polk went on to become the eleventh president of the United States, in 1844.

A Profile . . .

In 1843, at the age of 65, when he was the subject of a profile in a book on naval history, the commodore was described as ... "five feet nine inches

Charles Stewart; from a lithograph at the Naval Academy, Annapolis.

in height, erect and well proportioned, of a dignified and engaging presence, and possessed of great constitutional powers to endure hardships and privations of all kinds. His hair is of a chestnut colour; his eyes blue, large, penetrating, and intelligent."

As it continues, the profile becomes more revealing about the man behind those eyes . . . "Stewart possesses great vigour of mind, a high sense of justice, and inflexible resolution of purpose. His control over his passions is truly surprising; and under the most irritating circumstances, his oldest seamen have never yet seen a ray of anger flash from his eye. His kindness, benevolence and humanity are proverbial amongst those who know him; but his sense of justice and of the requisitions of duty are as unbending as fate."

... And the Reality

These comments were made at a time when Charles Stewart still had 25 years of life left to him. Perhaps the eulogy is too rich in content and is not objective enough, but what can be said about Stewart is that in addition to being a great seaman and natural leader, he had a deep sense of honour and humanity.

These traits are mentioned in a separate profile, where Stewart is said to have abhorred the English practice of impressment, particularly when those being impressed were American citizens being taken into Royal Navy service. This was one of the causes which precipitated the War of 1812. On at least two occasions, he rescued American victims of this nefarious practice.

End of Service

Effectively retired from active service, Stewart was in charge of the Philadelphia Navy Yard from 1838 to 1841, again in 1846, returning to the post in 1854 and remaining there until 1861. He was promoted to senior commodore in 1856, but the following year had to remind those in authority that there was still some fight left in the old sea dog.

In 1857, a change in navy regulations removed his name from the active naval lists. He at once wrote to Congress asking them to reinstate him. He reminded them that the officials of the City of New York and the State of Pennsylvania "honored me by marked expressions of praise, and that the Congress of the United States, by a resolution adopted on the 22nd of February 1816, requested the President to present me a gold medal, with suitable emblems and devices, in testimony of the high sense entertained by Congress of my gallantry, good conduct, and services." His appeal was successful and he was reinstated.

His Sword for a Pen

In 1859 Charles Stewart was created senior flag officer, by act of Congress, and in 1861, he felt obliged to resort to his pen yet again, beseeching the Department of the Navy to put him on active service in the Civil War. It is perhaps not surprising that they politely declined his offer, as he was 83 years old!

In another letter he claimed that the Civil War had not been caused by Northern intransigence, but by a determination of the South to remain in the Union only for so long as they were able to control democracy in their interest. The force of his writing and the skill of his arguments made certain the letter was one of three published in a pamphlet which enjoyed a wide circulation at the time.

Some six months before the Civil War began, Delia, the wife from whom he had been estranged for over 35 years, died while visiting their daughter in Ireland. Two years later, in 1862, when Charles Stewart retired, President Abraham Lincoln conferred on him the title of rear-admiral, the highest rank in the American Navy. He was to live out the rest of his life on his estate at Bordentown, where he died on 6 November 1869, aged 91.

His body was placed aboard a vessel and carried to Philadelphia, to be buried where he had wished, on the banks of the Schuylkill River, where his boyhood dreams of a mariner's life had first been stirred. The city of his birth - the place forever associated with independence and liberty - was to provide the fitting final resting place.

The residents of Bordentown and Fieldsboro generally recognised that their country had lost one of its most distinguished naval heroes, and their presence was represented by the Mayor, the council, and the many mourners who accompanied Commodore Stewart's remains to Independence Hall where thousands paid their respects while the Liberty Bell tolled its solemn notes.

On 7 November 1869, he was buried in Woodlawn Cemetery, in a grave which lies to the right of the old gates, opposite the University of Pennsylvania.

Return to "Ironsides"

Twenty years earlier, he had sold some of his land in order to settle $10,000 on each of his two legitimate children, Delia and Charles. With his passing, the residue of his estate was inherited jointly by them.

At the time of his death, Stewart had been attempting to eject the New Jersey and Amboy Railway from part of his land. The company had built some unsightly houses and sheds there and when Delia and Charles inherited the estate they settled the dispute by arbitration; the company being forced to remove all traces of the buildings near the house. Stewart had made a fortune in the merchant marine and had received substantial sums for the enemy ships he captured during the wars with the Barbary pirates and later in the War of 1812. However, he had put vast amounts of money into his presidency campaign, as well as into his estate over the years. He had a second family for which he had to provide, and his investments were also reduced by "Black Friday", in 1869, and again in 1873.

When her father died, Delia Parnell went to America with her younger children and lived at "Ironsides". She eventually leased the estate to a manual training and industrial school for black children, when she returned to Ireland. The estate was duly purchased for $15,000 by the State of New Jersey. The mansion house was torn down and replaced by an administration building which still stands. In 1953 the old industrial school was converted to the Johnstone Training and Research Centre for the mentally handicapped.

Charles Tudor Stewart

The only legitimate son of Admiral Stewart, Charles Tudor Stewart, played an unobtrusive yet influential part in the lives of many of the major characters in the story of the Stewarts and the Parnells.

He was always very close to Delia - "this almost twin sister" - and in later life, when she was widowed, he was a generous benefactor and sound advisor to her and her children.

Having worked first as an engineer for the Reading Railway, he studied law and went on to practise in New Orleans for many years. Through his friendship with Prince Lucien Murat, while he was a young man in Bordentown, Charles won a lucrative timber contract with the French navy. His wealth from this enabled him to live permanently in Paris.

At the time of the Admiral's foray into politics, Charles had become involved with a young woman and, when he introduced her to his sister, Delia was not impressed with his choice, straightaway writing to her father on what she believed "a very important subject": "I have seen Miss Bruce, and so far, do not consider her equal to Charles; five hundred thousand dollars might be worthy of him, but I should like a very superior, amiable person in addition." Going on to criticise the young woman for her looks and her pedigree, she justified her meddling by thinking that her brother did not have "much vocation" for marriage.

Charles remained a rich bachelor and was, therefore, the ideal brother and uncle in later years. In addition to helping his father, he had political aspirations of his own, and it is quite likely that he influenced Charles Stewart Parnell to go into politics, when his nephew stayed with him for a while in Paris in the late 1860s and early 1870s.

With the collapse of Jay Cooke and Company in America in 1873, Charles Tudor Stewart lost much of his fortune. Shortly after that he went to Rome, where he contracted typhus. He died there, in April 1874, aged 56.

Eleven

His Other Legacy

Admiral Stewart did, however, leave another legacy; his passionate loathing of injustice destined to ferment through one generation before manifesting itself in three of his grandchildren in far off County Wicklow: Charles Stewart Parnell, and his sisters, Fanny and Anna.

Although possibly not as colourful as some of the Admiral's exploits, the history of the children's family on the Parnell side over several generations was no less impressive. Their great-grandfather, the second Sir John Parnell, had sacrificed his position as Chancellor of the Irish Exchequer rather than accept the Act of Union which William Pitt was determined to pass through Parliament. Sir John's son, Henry (later created Baron Congleton) had written a history of the Penal Laws against the Irish Catholics, and had supported the Roman Catholic Relief Bill, in 1829 (thereby allowing Daniel O'Connell to sit in the House.) Sir John's other son, William Parnell, was a man of great compassion and social conscience. In 1819 he wrote a controversial novel *Maurice and Berghetta*, which advocated the recognition of Catholic civil rights and the improvement of Irish rural life. The book was dedicated to "the priesthood of Ireland", whose social function he endorsed, although he had little time for Roman Catholicism. Bearing in mind that the Parnells were essentially a family of Protestant landowners, their outspokenness was all the more unusual.

The influence of both William Parnell and Admiral Charles Stewart was to become inspirational to their grandchildren, preparing them for the stand they took against the mightiest power in the world, that of the Empire of

Queen Victoria, built as it was on the unconscionable greed of the Landed Gentry.

From the Meeting of the Waters . . .

In County Wicklow, the river Avonmore winds its way through quiet woodland before reaching Rathdrum, the village on a high ridge looking down on the valley of the Meeting of the Waters - immortalised in verse by Thomas Moore. It was to this idyllic setting, to nearby Avondale, that John Henry Parnell brought his young bride in 1835.

For all that Delia Parnell spent many of her formative years with her mother, she appears not to have learned much from the experience. When she married Parnell and travelled to Ireland she had little idea of what to expect when she got there. Earlier, after Parnell had proposed to her she told his travelling companion, Lord Powerscourt: "I don't like being lost in an Irish fog and I am afraid he has no house there."

However, Parnell's perseverance won her over, but if her mother had found herself isolated in New Jersey, Delia must have felt even more remote in Ireland. (Her daughter Emily was later to write of "the sudden transformation" Delia had undergone in coming to the solitude of Avondale from having been "the belle of New York.")

Delia endured eleven confinements on a fairly regular basis; beginning in 1836 and culminating in 1853; nine of her children being born at Avondale, one (Theodosia) in Torquay, England, and one (Henry) in Paris.

Like her mother, Delia lost her first child - coincidentally also called William - although not in infancy, but when he was five years old. The similarities did not end there, but in the case of Delia Parnell it was not until much later that she grew distant from her husband. (This was as a result of the death of their second son Hayes, following a riding accident.)

Later she recalled that her mother was opposed to her marrying Parnell until he promised to send her to America every year to see her family. "But," she said, "he did not keep his promise, as he did not promise to bring the children and I was not willing to leave them."

There were many inconsistencies about the character of Delia; for one who had daughters presented at Queen Victoria's court and dined in the viceregal circle at Dublin Castle, she was in a few years to espouse the ideals of Fenianism. She was seen by one contemporary as having a "strong American love of independence and a hearty hate of British greed and desire for domination."

. . . *To the Parting of the Ways*

When John Henry Parnell died suddenly in Dublin, in July 1859, Delia was in Paris visiting her brother. Parnell left a will which was to cause great bitterness in his wife and rancour among his children. Shortly after this, his widow was forced to let out Avondale, while she and her children moved to the town of Dalkey, some thirty miles from Avondale, and ten from Dublin. (Such were her feelings of uncharitableness towards her late husband, that later, when Delia lived with her brother Charles in Paris, she preferred the status of being the daughter of a famous American admiral, rather than the widow of an untitled Irish landowner.)

Within a year the family had moved again, this time to Kingstown, (now Dun Laoghaire), some six miles south of Dublin. It was while they were staying here that Delia Stewart, on a visit from America, died suddenly, in September 1860.

Charles Stewart Parnell

How apt it was that Charles Stewart Parnell should share the name of his heroic grandfather. The names William, Hayes, and John had already been used, acknowledging Parnell ancestors, but the birth of her fourth son gave Delia the opportunity to honour her kin. (It is generally assumed that Parnell was named after his grandfather, but Tudor family papers suggest that the choice of name honoured his uncle, Charles Tudor Stewart.)

His American association was not limited to his name; the Home Rule M.P. T.P. O'Connor later recorded, in his *Memoirs of an Old Parliamentarian*, that he had "always held that both in appearance and to a large extent in character (Charles Stewart) Parnell was much more American than either English or Irish."

From the outset both of his parents encouraged the young Charles to integrate fully - as much with the children of the estate workers as with those of the neighbouring gentrified families. He received most of his formal education in England, being first sent to a girls' school in Yeovil, Somerset

Charles Stewart Parnell, grandson of Charles Stewart and imbued with similar spirit.

- its choice said to have been in order "to put manners on him". Here he suffered a spell of typhoid, and eventually had to return home. After a year or so, he was again sent away, to a school near Kirk Langley, Derbyshire. He stayed there for a year.

He was subsequently educated at home up to the time of his father's death, in 1859. After that he went to a school in Chipping Norton, Oxfordshire, in order to cram before being admitted to Magdalene College, Cambridge.

In May 1869 Parnell was rusticated from Cambridge, and returned home. In 1870, following the death of Admiral Stewart, Delia Parnell went to

Bordentown, and in the spring of 1871 Charles Stewart Parnell visited America, ostensibly to pursue the affections of an American girl he had met in Paris. Unlike his father before him, he was unsuccessful in his quest.

Parnell Enters Politics

According to a statement he made in 1889, Parnell cited the passing of the Ballot Act in 1872 as "the first public event which more intimately directed my attention to politics."

After failing to secure nomination for the Wicklow seat in 1874, he stood for the County of Dublin in the same year, but was roundly beaten. It was the following year before he was successful, and took his seat in the House of Commons, as M.P. for Meath, and joined the Home Rule party led by Isaac Butt.

In 1877 Parnell began the exercise of obstructionism in the House, a practice which had been used before, but now he took it further and used it in issues which had no bearing on Irish politics, as evidenced by his causing a 26-hour sitting on the South Africa Bill. Later that year he was elected President of the Home Rule Confederation of Great Britain.

With a run of poor harvests in the late 1870s, there was a decrease in demand for agricultural produce, leading to a fall in prices and an upsurge in agrarian agitation. In October 1879 the Irish National Land League was founded by Michael Davitt, and he invited Parnell to become its president.

Just as impressment and abuses of liberty had fired Admiral Stewart's belligerency, the issue which united his grandchildren was that of landlordism. Parnell saw the destruction of this feudal parasitism as merely a step towards the overthrow of British rule in Ireland and accepted the offer. In the autumn of 1880 his sister Fanny started the Ladies' Land League in America, and the following year its work was extended to Ireland, their younger sister Anna taking charge.

Parnell and Mrs. O'Shea

In May 1880 Parnell was elected chairman of the Irish Parliamentary Party and two months later he met Katharine O'Shea, the estranged wife of Captain William O'Shea, a member of his own party. She had married O'Shea in 1867 although her father, chaplain to Queen Caroline, had not approved of her marrying a Roman Catholic.

She began to visit the Ladies' Gallery in the House of Commons to hear him speak and a relationship developed between them. By the end of that year they had become so close that they spent Christmas together, at her home in Eltham, London.

In March 1881 the Protection of Person and Property (Ireland) Act was passed, this being the British government's coercive reaction to the agrarian agitation in Ireland. In August the Land Law (Ireland) Act was passed, with the purpose of stemming the land agitation. A month later Parnell urged the Land League Convention to "test the act", and on 13 October he was arrested and imprisoned in Kilmainham Jail.

At this time Katharine was expecting his child. She had the baby in February 1882, and when Parnell was given parole to attend the funeral of his nephew Henry (only son of his sister Delia) in Paris, he called to see Katharine. The baby, Claude Sophie, was ill and dying. When she died, on 22 April, Parnell had returned to prison. An agreement - the Kilmainham Treaty - was reached with the British shortly after this, and on 2 May Parnell was released, after serving seven months.

Divorce and Marriage

Katharine had two further children by him, but it was not until 1890 that she finally got her divorce from Captain O'Shea. The divorce proceedings began shortly after an official enquiry cleared Parnell of complicity in murder during the land war (the Phoenix Park Murders). The allegations were made by a newspaperman named Pigott, who broke down under cross-examination (and later committed suicide.) Parnell cleared his name of the allegations, only to face bitter opposition at home for his part in an undefended divorce scandal.

Katharine married Parnell in 1891 and in the September of that year he made his final public speech, at Creggs, County Roscommon. He returned to Katharine, in Brighton, totally worn out. He died there on the 6th October 1891.

His body was returned to Ireland on Sunday 11 October, to be buried at Glasnevin Cemetery. A great boulder of Wicklow granite marks his resting-place, on it the single word PARNELL.

The monument erected in his memory in O'Connell Street, Dublin, quotes from one of his speeches: "No man has a right to fix the boundary to the march of a nation. No man has a right to say to his country: 'Thus far shalt thou go and no further.' We have never attempted to fix the *ne plus ultra* to the progress of Ireland's nationhood and we never shall."

Charles Stewart Parnell - 27 June 1846 - 6 October 1891.

Katharine O'Shea

Parnell wrote a poem for Katharine which was published in her book *Charles Stewart Parnell: his love-story and political life*:

> The grass shall cease to grow,
> The river's stream to run,
> The stars shall ponder in their course,
> No more shall shine the sun;
> The moon shall never wane or grow,
> The tide shall cease to ebb and flow,
> Ere I shall cease to love you.

Katharine O'Shea; Parnell had this photograph with him in Kilmainham Jail.

Fanny Parnell

Fanny was the sister of whom Parnell was particularly fond. By her early teens she was becoming an accomplished poet, contributing poems on a regular basis to the *Irish People*, most showing her social conscience. By the time she accompanied her mother to America in 1874, she had become increasingly involved in politics and went on to found the American Ladies' Land League.

William O'Brien, editor of *United Ireland* and one of Charles Stewart Parnell's closest allies, described Fanny as "one with all the Promethean

Fanny Parnell, founder of the Ladies' Land League.

passion and the Promethean unhappiness of the poet." *Hold the Harvest*, first published in 1880, was the poem which made her name famous. An article in the *Edinburgh Review* on the subject of Irish discontent pinpointed her poetry as a major cause of national unrest.

She suffered from poor health and, when she died in America in 1882, aged 33, it was generally assumed that her remains would be transported back to Ireland for interment. Her brother Charles was totally opposed to this and, as a result, other arrangements had to be made. Her Tudor relatives offered their family vault at Mount Auburn, Cambridge, Massachusetts, as an immediate solution.

Her coffin was interred there, but, over the years, the matter of a final, permanent, place was discussed, and in the 1940s moves were made to have it shipped back to Ireland. In 2001, a compromise was reached, when a stone of Wicklow granite was transported to America by the Parnell Society and, one hundred and nineteen years after she died, Fanny Parnell's final resting place was agreed upon.

The stone of Wicklow granite commemorating Fanny Parnell's life.

Anna Parnell

Anna, sadly, was overshadowed, if not totally eclipsed, by her famous brother. Like Fanny, she was a poet and her outspoken unconventional social observations and political views outraged many. She is now generally regarded as the first truly prominent Irish woman politician of modern times.

She founded the Ladies' Land League in 1881, organised branches and distributed £60,000 in relief. Her brother Charles distrusted her deeper understanding of the political situation, and when she asked him for funds to discharge heavy debts, he gave the money on condition that the League be disbanded. This was done in 1882, but Anna never forgave him or saw him again.

In 1905, when William O'Brien wrote his memoirs, he had little doubt as to the importance of Anna, writing: "But the true militant leader of the Ladies' Land League, its inspiration and guiding force in action was Miss

Anna Parnell, seated at desk, in the office of the Ladies' Land League.

Anna Parnell, a sister of the Irish leader, who, it is not too much to say, was, in more than one respect, little removed in genius from her brother."

In later life she seems to have become deranged, and was drowned in Ifracombe, Devon, in 1911, after entering a rough sea despite warnings.

Avondale . . . after the Parnells

Delia Parnell divided her later years between her two homes, returning to Avondale in 1891, in 1894, and finally in 1896, after leasing out "Ironsides". She lived at Avondale until her death in March 1898. She died as a result of the burns she received after a spark from the fire in her bedroom set her clothes alight. She is buried in Glasnevin Cemetery, Dublin.

Deep in debt, her son John Howard Parnell sold Avondale the same year, to one William Boylan, on the understanding that he could buy it back two years later. However, he could never meet Boylan's price and when Boylan died in 1904 the estate was bought by the Department of Agriculture, the intention being to start a forestry school there. The connection was an obvious one, since Avondale had been extensively planted, first by Samuel Hayes, in 1779. Charles Stewart Parnell also had a great interest in developing it as a source of local employment and had built his own sawmill there.

Avondale House was occupied by British soldiers at one time and, after the truce, by soldiers of the Free State. With the foundation of the State, the Department of Agriculture took over Avondale, where the training of apprentices continued. An arboretum and pinetum were also laid down, containing a wide range of exotic trees and shrubs. Avondale was to become known as the "cradle of Irish forestry".

Although the school ceased in the 1970s, Avondale House continued to be used for in-service training and also became the local Forest Office. In 1989 *Coillte Teoranta* (The Irish Forestry Board) was formed and a refurbishment programme was begun in order to open it to the public by 1991, the centenary of Parnell's death.

Now the house, set in its magnificent grounds, and with trees planted by Hayes and the Parnells still standing, attracts visitors from all over the world.

Delia Tudor Parnell, in 1864.

Twelve

"Old Ironsides": Man & Ship

In 1880, when Charles Stewart Parnell became known as the "uncrowned King of Ireland", some patriotic Irish-Americans found a neat juxtaposition, by referring to the victory his grandfather had over the British 65 years earlier. They tried to attribute to the Admiral anti-British feelings which he did not necessarily hold.

Admiral Charles Stewart was born in America, a choice of country made for him by his immigrant parents. His first love, as Delia had learned to her chagrin, was the sea. He lived for the sea, in war and in peace. In retrospect, what can be said of the man is that he fought the British just as he had fought the French, the Tripolitans, and the Algerians before them, with no more passion and no less aggression.

It was true he detested the British Navy for their impressment policy, but to him an enemy was an enemy as long as a threat existed, and he was quick to offer help, or in some cases a conciliatory glass, to a vanquished foe.

Charles Stewart was justifiably famous for being a great sea captain, and for his brief but memorable association with the ***Constitution***. His court martial, the effect that it had on his career, his marriage, and his children, must be largely, if not wholly, attributed to his wife's rashness.

Although Delia was privy to a side of his nature unseen by others, and was, at the time of their separation, exposed to his "cold, implacable anger", it would seem that she brought much of that upon herself.

In judging Charles Stewart in how he performed his duty and did his chosen work, it should be noted that in almost thirty years of naval service, when he saw as much fighting as any of his contemporaries, he never struck his colours, or lost a ship. (And the list of his contemporaries who did includes William Bainbridge, David Porter, James Barron, James Lawrence, and Oliver Hazard Perry.)

It is, therefore, fitting that he should have achieved his most famous victory aboard the ship that has been immortalised by its durability, and has withstood the pounding of storms, battles, and, most of all, the sea ...

*The **Constitution**; from a contemporary engraving published in Boston.*

Constituents of the Constitution

The man who built the ***Constitution*** to Joshua Humphreys' plan was George Claghorn. He had first been attracted to the port of New Bedford in Bristol County when there was a whaling industry there.

The white oak timbers used in her construction were cut in the forests near the town of Whitman in Plymouth County, and were squared in the local mills.

The original sails for the *Constitution* were made in the Old Granary Building on the corner of Boston's Tremont and Park Streets. In 1809 the Congregational Church was built on the site.

Originally intended to carry 44 guns, the number and size of the *Constitution*'s ordnance changed in the several refits she underwent over the years. She was fitted with long 24-pounders on her 175-foot gun-deck, and long 12-pounders on her forecastle and quarter-deck. With an overall length of 204 feet, she was 1,444 American tons (1,533 British) and displaced 2,200 tons. At her launch in 1797 her ochre hull was embellished with a figurehead of Hercules mounting the rock of Independence, clutching the Constitution in one hand, the classic fasces in the other. Just before the war of 1812 she was refitted, returning with a new billet head, dragon-encrusted trail board, star-studded stern decorations, together with a battery of twenty-two 32-pounder carronades on her spar deck.

The *Constitution* fought in over forty engagements without suffering any serious damage.

The Constitution: The Poets' Friend

In 1815, while Captain Charles Stewart, his officers, and crew were being fêted in their different ways, the *Constitution* was laid up in Boston, where she would stay for the next six years. On 13 May 1821, she sailed as the flagship of Commodore Jacob Jones in the Mediterranean.

Lord Byron, at that time "probably the most famous Englishman in Europe", visited the ship on this cruise. At that time Byron was supporting the Greek insurgents' attempt to liberate their country from centuries of Turkish oppression.

The *Constitution* returned to Boston in 1823, where she remained until 1826, when she once again went back to the Mediterranean. Byron had died in 1824, still fighting for Greek liberation, but it was during this cruise that "Old Ironsides" was summoned to aid Byron's starving Greek insurgents in recovering a large cargo of provisions that had been stolen.

She returned to Boston in July 1828, went out of commission, and the following year was surveyed and reported unseaworthy. The estimated cost of repairs exceeded the total original cost of building the ship, and the decision was taken to break her up or sell her off.

Oliver Wendell Holmes (1809-94) wrote many poems about ships and the sea, but he is best known for *"Old Ironsides"*. He wrote this in 1830, when he learned that the ship was to be scrapped.

> Aye, tear her tattered ensign down!
>   Long has it waved on high,
> And many an eye has danced to see
>   That banner in the sky;
> Beneath it rung the battle shout,
>   And burst the cannon's roar;
> The meteor of the ocean's air
>   Shall sweep the clouds no more!
>
> Her deck, once red with heroes' blood,
>   Where knelt the vanquished foe,
> When winds were hurrying o'er the flood
>   And waves were white below,
> No more shall feel the victor's tread,
>   Or know the conquered knee;
> The harpies of the shore shall pluck
>   The eagle of the sea!
>
> O better that her shattered hulk
>   Should sink beneath the wave;
> Her thunders shook the mighty deep,
>   And there should be her grave;
> Nail to the mast her holy flag,
>   Set her every threadbare sail,
> And give her to the god of storms,
>   The lightning and the gale.

In Service Again . . .

The great wave of patriotic sentiment that swept the country as the poem was reprinted in almost every newspaper reprieved her. Congress quickly voted on the matter and the funds were found. The old ship was the first vessel to be taken into the new dry dock just completed at the Boston Navy Yard.

It was found that her keel was raised and two and a half feet out of alignment, the probable result of her having stuck on the ways at her launching. After a complete restoration, she was ready for a relaunch in 1834. It was while she was here that her figurehead - a full-length figure of President Andrew Jackson - was decapitated, by one, Samuel Dewey.

After the *Constitution* went to New York, the figurehead was repaired, and remained in situ for the next forty years before being removed and placed in the Naval Academy at Annapolis.

The *Constitution* was back in service again, and served as the flagship of many commodores, and went to the Mediterranean and the Pacific. Commodore Stewart was reunited with her between 1841-43, before he returned to Philadelphia and she was sent on a special cruise to the China seas, under Captain "Mad Jack" Percival. After circumnavigating the globe, she returned home around Cape Horn, reaching Boston on 5 October 1848. She had sailed 52,279 miles in 495 days at sea, an average of 106 miles a day.

She was laid up for a couple of years, then after another two tours to the Mediterranean and cruising on the coast of Africa, she returned to Portsmouth, New Hampshire, in 1854, and was taken out of commission, never again to put to sea on active naval service.

In April 1861, at the outbreak of the Civil War, Captain George Blake, superintendent of the Naval Academy at Annapolis, feared that the Maryland secessionists planned to attack the academy. He embarked the faculty and the midshipmen on the *Constitution*, and sailed for New York. The academy relocated at Newport, Rhode Island, for the duration of the war, while the academy yard in Annapolis was transformed into an army hospital.

And so to England . . .

After the war "Old Ironsides" returned to Annapolis and, in 1871, went to the yard at Philadelphia to be repaired for the Centennial Exposition of 1876, but she was not ready when the time came. However, in March 1878, she was used to transport goods to the Paris Exposition. After remaining nine months at Le Havre, she sailed for home, but on the night of 16 January 1879, she ran aground on the English coast off Ballard's Point.

The British authorities sent a steam battleship to assist in getting their redoubtable old enemy afloat again, and she was docked at Portsmouth. She stayed there for two weeks, but her proverbial good fortune seemed to have deserted her, for in a heavy gale two weeks later, she twisted her rudder-head off, and was forced to run before the wind for Lisbon. Eventually she reached New York on 24 May.

The Constitution Comes Home

She again became a training ship for the academy, cruising in the West Indies in winter, and up to Nova Scotia in summer. In 1882 she was taken out of commission and sent to New York as a receiving ship.

In response to a request from the citizens of Boston, she was ordered back to her native city for the centennial anniversary of her launch. She arrived there on 21 September 1897, and the entire North Atlantic fleet including the **New York, Brooklyn, Iowa, Massachusetts,** and **Texas**, were anchored in the harbour to welcome "Old Ironsides".

The great celebrations in the city at the time were likened to those other patriotic demonstrations some eighty years before, when Captains Hull, Bainbridge, and Stewart returned home in victory.

Just after the turn of the century, Professor Ira N. Hollis wrote an exhaustive book "The Frigate ***Constitution***", and he ended it thus:

"The old craft now lies housed over and tenantless, except for the crowd of memories which people her decks. She has reached another stage in her existence demanding the assistance of every lover of his country to secure for her a long lease of life. By an Act of Congress, approved February 14, 1900, the Secretary of the Navy is authorized to restore her to the same condition as regards her hull and rigging as she was when in active service; provided that a sufficient sum of money to complete the work shall be raised through the agency of the Massachusetts State Society of the United States Daughters of 1812. The amount required is estimated at $400,000, and the patriotic women having the business in charge will no doubt realize their hopes of seeing the old ship completely restored in the course of a few years."

Professor Hollis was right in his assessment of the dedication of the "Daughters"; they reached their financial target and the ship was rebuilt in 1906. Since her first massive rebuilding operation in the 1830s, the ***Constitution*** was rebuilt between the years 1871-77, again in 1906, and for the last time between 1927-30.

Even to this Day . . .

During the celebrations of the bicentenary of the American Declaration of Independence she was brought out for a brief sail around the harbour from which she first sailed nearly 200 years before. She is the oldest commissioned warship afloat. Still a feature of Boston Harbour, in 1997 she was refurbished, and is now a major tourist attraction and is used for corporate events.

*"**Old Ironsides**" in Charlestown Harbour, Boston, with the Bunker Hill Monument (its building first suggested by William Tudor Jr.) in the background.*

His Name Lived On

In 1898, just over a hundred years after Charles Stewart was appointed First Lieutenant on the *United States*, authorisation was given by Congress for the building of the first group of true U.S. torpedo boat destroyers. These were patterned after existing foreign models, and were all named after the early commodores: DD1 being the *Bainbridge*, DD5 the *Decatur*, etc. They could carry a crew of 75, and had a speed of 29 knots.

The *Stewart* was built by the Gas Engine & Power Company of Morris Heights, and was commissioned on 17 December 1902. She was eventually sold out of service on 3 January 1920. A later destroyer, *Stewart* (DD 224), served in World War II in the Pacific, and was badly damaged in the Battle of the Badung Strait in February 1942.

©   Colin Stewart, 2001

           Jean Costelloe, 2001

Appendix

Minutes of the action between the United States' frigate ***Constitution***, and his Britannic majesty's ships ***Cyane*** and ***Levant***, on the 20th February, 1815.

Commences with light breezes from the east, and cloudy weather. At one, discovered a sail two points on the larboard bow - hauled up and made sail in chase. At a quarter past one, made the sail to be a ship; at three-quarters past one, discovered an other sail ahead; made them out at two P.M. to be both ships, standing close hauled, with their starboard tacks on board; at 4 P.M. the weather most ship made signals, and bore up to her consort, then about 10 miles to leeward; we bore up after her, and set lower top-mast, top-gallant, and royal studding sails in chase; at half-past 4, carried away our main royal mast; took in the sails and got another prepared; at 5 P.M. commenced firing on the chase from our two larboard bow guns; our shot falling short, ceased firing; at half-past five, finding it impossible to prevent their junction, cleared ship for action, then about four miles from the two ships; at 40 minutes after 5, they passed within hail of each other, and hauled by the wind on the starboard tack, hauled up their courses, and prepared to receive us; at forty-five minutes past five, they made all sail close hauled by the wind, in hopes of getting to the windward of us; at 55 minutes past 5, finding themselves disappointed in their object, and we were closing with them fast, they shortened sail, and formed on a line of wind, about half a cable's length from each other. At 6 P.M. having them under command of our battery, hoisted our colours, which was answered by both ships hoisting English ensigns. At 5 minutes past 6, ranged up on the starboard side of the sternmost ship, about 300 yards distant, and commenced the action by broadsides, both ships returning our fire with the greatest spirit for about 15 minutes, then the fire of the enemy beginning to slacken, and the great column of smoke collected under our lee, induced us to cease our fire to ascertain their positions and conditions. In about three minutes the smoke clearing away, we found ourselves abreast of the headmost ship, the sternmost ship luffing up for our larboard quarter; we poured a broadside into the headmost ship, and braced aback our main and mizen topsails, and backed astern under cover of the smoke, abreast with the sternmost ship, when the action was continued with spirit and considerable effect, until 35 minutes past 6, when the enemy's fire again slackened, and we discovered the headmost bearing up; filled our topsails, shot ahead, and gave her two stern rakes. We then discovered the sternmost ship wearing also; wore ship immediately after her, and gave a stern rake, she luffing to on our starboard bow, and giving us her larboard broadside. We ranged upon her larboard quarter, within hail, and was about to give her our starboard broadside, when she struck her colours, fired a lee gun and yielded. At 50 minutes past 6, took possession of his Britannic majesty's ship ***Cyane***, captain Gordon Falcon, mounting 34 guns. At 8 P.M. filled away after her consort, which was still in sight to leeward. At half past 8, found her standing towards us, with her starboard tacks close hauled, with topgallant sails set and colours flying. At 50 minutes past 8, ranged close alongside to windward of her, on opposite tacks, and exchanged broadsides; wore immediately under her stern and raked with a broadside.

She then crowded all sail and endeavoured to escape by running; hauled on board our tacks, set spanker and flying jib in chase. At half past 9, commenced firing on her from our starboard bow chaser; gave her several shot, which cut her spars and rigging considerably. At 10 P.M. finding they could not escape, fired a gun, struck her colours, and yielded. We immediately took possession of his Britannic majesty's ship ***Levant***, hon. captain George Douglass, mounting 21 guns. At 1 A.M. the damages of our rigging were repaired, sails shifted, and the ship in fighting condition.

(Copied verbatim from minutes enclosed with Captain Stewart's letter to the Secretary of the Navy, May 1815.)

Glossary

Brig: Sailing vessel having two square-rigged masts and additional lower fore-and-aft sail with a gaff and boom on the mainmast.

Cruise: Sail in specified area for protection of shipping.

Flotilla: Small fleet; fleet of boats or small ships.

Frigate: Formerly, a ship having a single enclosed gun deck. (The upper deck would also hold a number of guns, but was not counted as a gun deck.) American ships were designed to carry from 28 to 44 guns, whereas British models could carry between 28 and 60 guns.

Indiaman: Ship engaged in trade with India or the East Indies, especially.

Kedge: To change position of vessel by winding in hawser attached to small anchor at some distance.

Ketch: Small two-masted or cutter-rigged coasting vessel.

Knot: Unit of speed of one nautical mile per hour (originally measured by knots on log-line). A nautical mile is the length of one minute of latitude, standardised at 6,080 feet.

Luff: To bring ship's head nearer wind; turn helm so as to secure this.

Master Commandant:	An obsolete naval rank, between lieutenant and captain, replaced in American navy by that of commander in 1838.
Polacre:	(Or polacca) A three-masted, Mediterranean vessel on which the foremast is lateen-rigged and the main and mizen-mast square-rigged.
Privateer:	Armed vessel owned and operated by private persons holding commission from government (letters of marque) and authorized to use it against a hostile power, especially in capture of merchant shipping.
Schooner:	A sailing vessel with two or more masts rigged fore-and-aft, usually carrying two or more topsails.
Ship:	In sailing terms, a vessel with bowsprit (spar running out from ship's stem, to which forestays are fastened) and three square-rigged masts, each divided into lower, top, and topgallant mast.
Ship of the line:	Naval sailing vessels were divided into six classes according to the number of guns carried. The first three classes, vessels thought powerful enough to take their place in the line of battle, were called ships of the line. They had two or three gundecks and carried at least 64 guns.
Sloop:	A small sailing vessel having a single mast rigged fore-and-aft.
Sloop of war:	A term used to describe any small, cruising naval vessel, regardless of her rig, carrying fewer guns than a frigate, usually under 20
Strike colours:	To lower flag, thereby signal surrender.
Tack:	To pursue course obliquely opposed to the direction of the wind.
Wear:	To put ship about by turning head away from wind.

Bibliography

Bew, Paul; The Life of C.S. Parnell; Gill and MacMillan, Dublin, 1980.

Bowen, Catherine Drinker; John Adams and the American Revolution; Little, Brown, & Co., Boston, 1950.

Brannan, John, ed.; The First American Frontier: Official Letters of the Military and Naval Officers of the United States, during the War with Great Britain in the years 1812,13,14 and 15. Arno Press & *The New York Times*, 1970. Originally published in 1823.

Coletta, Paolo E.; American Secretaries of the Navy, Volume 1, 1775-1913; Naval Institute Press, Annapolis.

Cooper, James Fennimore; The History of the United States Navy, Volume I & II; Richard Bentley, London, 1839.

Côté, Jane McL.; Fanny & Anna Parnell; Macmillan, London 1991.

Frost, John; Lives of the Commodores of the United States Navy; Nafis & Cornish, New York, 1845.

Guttridge, Leonard F, & Jay D Smith; The Commodores - The U.S. Navy in the Age of Sail; Harper & Row, New York, 1969.

Harding, J; Biographical Sketch and Services of Commodore Charles Stewart of the United States Navy; Philadelphia, 1838.

Hill, Frederic Stanhope; Twenty Six Historic Ships; G.P. Putnam's Sons, Knickerbocker Press, New York, 1903.

Hollis, Ira N.; The Frigate "*Constitution*".

Kee, Robert; The Laurel and the Ivy; Hamish Hamilton, London, 1993.

Lyons, F.S.L.; Charles Stewart Parnell; Collins, London, 1977.

Mahan, Captain A.T.; Sea Power in its relations to the War of 1812, Volume I & II; Sampson, Low, Marston & Co., London, 1905.

Morris, James M.; History of the U.S. Navy; Bison Books, London, 1984.

Pratt, Fletcher; The Compact History of the United States Navy, 1962.

Spears, John R; History of the United States Navy 1775-1897, Volume 3; Bickers & Son, 1898.

Sweetman, Jack; American Naval History; an Illustrated Chronology of the U.S. Navy and Marine Corps, 1775-Present; Naval Institute Press, Annapolis, 1984.

Webster's Biographical Dictionary; G & C Merriam, Springfield, Massachusetts, 1974.

Other Bibliographical Sources

Death of Fanny Parnell; *Bordentown Register*, 28 July 1882.

Historic Bordentown; Florence A. Magee; *Bordentown Register*, 17 May 1956.

Bordentown Tales; from *Bordentown (N.J.) Register*, 26 March 1964.

Bicentennial Briefs, No.6; Prepared by the Bicentennial Committee, Bordentown, 1976.